Paranormal America

Megan Moxon

ISBN: 1523794534
ISBN-13: 978-1523794539

CONTENT

INTRODUCTION

Dearest Readers,

Ever since I was fourteen years old and had my first paranormal experience, I have been itching for more information about what we don't understand.

I have had hundreds of people from all over the United States write in about their personal experiences. The responses were so exciting, overwhelming, and some extremely emotional.

These people are no different than you and I, and it has been such a pleasure to connect and share stories.

Although I can't verify all fifty of these stories are completely true, they are certainly interesting. I hope as you read this book you keep an open mind and heart about what these people have encountered.

Enjoy the stories,
■ *Megan Moxon*

ALABAMA

As told by: Vivien Bullard

There were no pre-warning signs of paranormal activity at my duplex. It all started the day I was moving in. I was alone, bringing in the first load of my personal belongings from my car.

I walked into the bedroom and the door slammed closed behind me. I went to open the door and it would not open. The door locking mechanism was jammed and I could not get the door to open. There was no way I could climb out the bedroom window; it was too far down to the ground to climb or jump out and my phone was in my purse in the living room.

I had to scream for help from the bedroom window until finally a neighbor not even from my duplex heard me and came to my rescue. Luckily the front door of my duplex was not locked so she was able to walk right in, but she could not open the bedroom door either. She had to get her husband to come over and take the door off the hinges in order for me to get out. We discussed what had happened and there were no windows open, the air conditioning was not on and there was no way to explain why the door slammed as I walked into the room. I had been moving in furniture the day before with friends and the door never closed like that. When my landlord came over the next day to re-hang the door, the door knob locking mechanism was working just fine. I did not have any other problems with the bedroom door. But, a few days after that...

I was sitting on the living room floor, talking on the phone and I saw a strange ball of light dart around the room very fast, then it disappeared. Right after that happened, a peanut M&M popped up out of the candy dish on the glass cocktail table. The M&M hit the glass table top and then fell to the floor. I was telling my friend on the phone what just happened and she said the light might have been an orb. She chuckled at me and said, "Maybe the spirit just wanted a piece of candy," but I had no idea what an orb was. So I started researching orbs and what I saw that day looked just like the balls of light in the pictures of orbs. I continued to see orbs, off and on for several days.

Then... one morning as I was getting dressed for work, I heard the sound of keys rattling. I walked into the living room, thinking that my landlord was unlocking my door and was going to just walk in. I was a bit startled thinking he would do something like that unannounced, but then I noticed my car keys were on the floor. My keys were inside my purse, and my purse was sitting on the couch. My purse did not move, there was nothing else that came out. Just my keys.

By now I am starting to get a little frustrated. When I got to work I called my landlord and asked him if any strange activity had ever been reported from this duplex, did someone die there, anything that might explain these strange things that were happening. He was not aware of anything and never had a tenant say that any unusual activity happened while they lived there.

So, I drive home from work that day and when I get to the side door that I always enter the house through, the porch light was on. I know I turned the porch light off before I left because it is a ritual of mine. I lived alone and I liked having the light on for security purposes at night. But I always turned the light off when I left each morning. I know I turned the light off, and it was on. I called my landlord to see if he had gone to the duplex while I was at work, he said no. My landlord was probably beginning to think that I was crazy and I was beginning to think that he was entering my apartment when I was not there. But even that could not explain the orbs and other moving objects.

As I walked into my kitchen, the same day as when the porch light was on, I noticed something unusual. Next to the kitchen sink on the countertop, I had a shell cherub on an acrylic stand. It was a unique piece like I had never seen before. A small solid white sea shell about the size of a plum with a baby cherub head made from some type of ceramic/porcelain affixed at the top of the flat side of the shell. I had bought it from a gift shop at the hospital when I had a miscarriage. It was sitting on a clear acrylic stand. The cherub shell was turned around completely, facing the wall. Okay, I live alone, I haven't had any visitors up to this point and I do not have a cat... I am a meticulous housekeeper so how did this thing get turned around like this? By this time, I am really thinking that my landlord is coming into my duplex when I am not at home and doing things like this to mess with me. I called him immediately and he just laughed at me. He said, he was not coming into the duplex and that I just needed to calm down.

Okay, I do not drink, I do not take drugs of any kind, I am not making this stuff up. But I am starting to realize that something is definitely wrong here...

I'm an easily scared type of person anyway - I don't even watch scary movies. I do not like living alone and even though this is a pretty good neighborhood, I'm starting to feel scared.

A few nights later as I was sleeping, I wake up in a fearful panic because I felt something tugging at the back of my T-shirt. I know I felt it, something pulled the back of my shirt and woke me up. I was not dreaming, it scared the crap out of me and woke me up. It was a strong pull like it was trying to pull me off of the bed. I tried to rationalize what just happened and think if there was some way that my shirt got caught on something, but there was nothing it could have gotten caught on. There was no way to rationalize this...

So, sleepy and frustrated I move from the bed to the futon couch in the living room. I finally doze off to sleep. The next morning, I am telling my co-workers about what happened with my T-shirt and several of them tell me that maybe I have a ghost in the house. I do not like ghosts or anything of that nature and I have signed a one-year lease at this duplex. I am feeling like my privacy is being violated and people are starting to think I am crazy.

A few days and nights pass and nothing happens. Until one night, I am sleeping on the futon because I am afraid to sleep in my bed. I have this very scary dream of a man's voice laughing out loud in a scary laugh and I am seeing myself being held up to the ceiling by some force that I cannot see. I am seeing myself flying up at the ceiling all around the living room. I fly around the perimeter of the living room, then I fly into the spare bedroom, flying along the edges of each room. I can see all of the things in each room just exactly the way they are situated in the room. I am asleep but it was almost like I was awake because I was aware that I was watching myself flying around the rooms. And the entire time I am flying around the rooms, this man's voice is laughing out loud in this scary way. It was as if I knew, in my asleep and somewhat awake mode that this man was making me do this. I wake up and I am mad, very upset, angry, and I cannot get back to

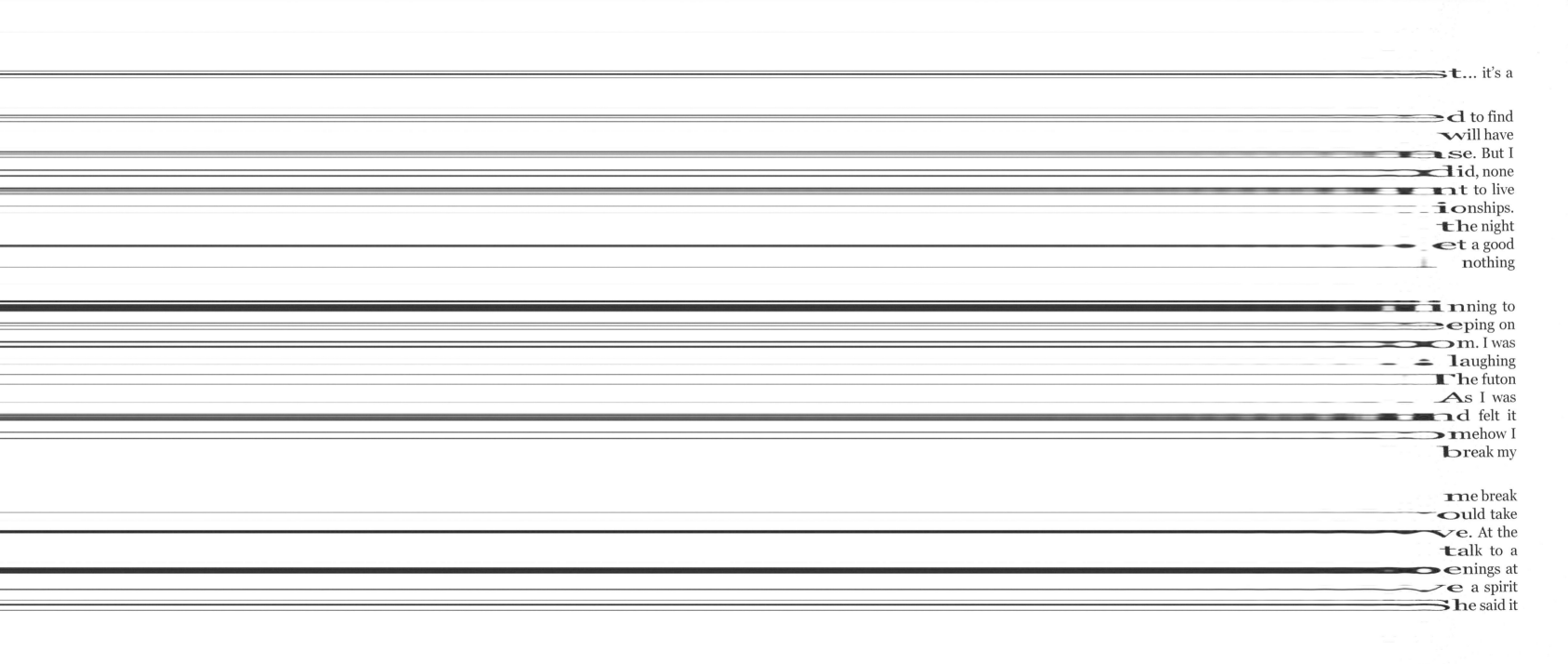

st... it's a

d to find
will have
se. But I
did, none
nt to live
ionships.
the night
et a good
nothing

nning to
eping on
om. I was
laughing
The futon
As I was
d felt it
mehow I
break my

me break
ould take
ve. At the
talk to a
enings at
e a spirit
She said it

was like Casper

Casper was not so

the night and that

psychic what her

get moved becaus

on my health an

She recommende

should not get at

could absorb the

don't like cats so

issue. She also sai

sea salt underne

mixture of herbs

leading to my car

to keep the spirit

cinnamon, sage an

psychic's home, I

mind the herbs an

a cat.

    The next

getting a cat. Do

especially dogs an

ago was my barn

feed and it never

freak and having

not for me. So I ge

did not even have

fearful of what the

the spirit and dyin

cat food, litter, litt

sleep. I am thinking... okay... I have a ghost... it's a man... and he is very annoying!

By now I am beginning to think I need to find a roommate for the spare bedroom, just so I will have someone around to help me feel more at ease. But I really do not want a roommate and even if I did, none of my good friends are in a position to want to live with me. They are either married, or in relationships. I might get a friend to come over and spend the night every now and then just so maybe I could get a good night's sleep. So that is what I did, and nothing happened when I had a friend stay over.

A few weeks passed and I was beginning to think my ghost had given up. I was still sleeping on the futon because I felt safer in the living room. I was sleeping and was awoken by the same man's laughing voice, but this time the futon was shaking. The futon was shaking underneath me, with force. As I was waking up, it was still moving, I saw and felt it moving. That was the last straw for me. Somehow I had to convince my landlord to allow me to break my lease. I was ready to move out.

My landlord reluctantly agreed to let me break my lease, but I knew realistically that it would take me a few weeks to find another place to live. At the recommendation of a friend, I went to talk to a psychic. I told the psychic about the happenings at the duplex and she told me that I did have a spirit there. Not a mean spirit, but a playful one. She said it was like Casper the friendly ghost. I told her that Casper was not so friendly waking me up all hours of the night and that I was planning to move. I asked the psychic what her advice was for me to do until I could get moved because the lack of sleep was taking a toll on my health and my work performance at my job. She recommended that I get a cat. She said that I should not get attached to the cat because the cat could absorb the energy of the spirit and die. Well, I don't like cats so getting attached to one was not an issue. She also said for me to put a bowl of water with sea salt underneath my bed. And to prepare a mixture of herbs to sprinkle on the floor out the door leading to my car as I was finally leaving the duplex to keep the spirit from following me. The herbs were cinnamon, sage and garlic cloves. As I was leaving the psychic's home, I was thinking over and over, I don't mind the herbs and the salt water, but I do not want a cat.

The next day, I am at the animal shelter, getting a cat. Don't get me wrong, I love animals, especially dogs and horses, but the only cat I had long ago was my barn cat that kept mice out of my horse feed and it never came inside the house. I am a neat freak and having a cat or dog inside the house is just not for me. So I get this calico cat, a spayed female. I did not even have the heart to name her because I was fearful of what the psychic said about her absorbing the spirit and dying. I spent all of this money getting cat food, litter, litter box, poop scoop, and a cat. That night I put the bowl of salt water under my bed and I think, great, tonight I am going to get some sleep. NOT! As soon as I fell asleep this cat woke me up meowing and running around the room, jumping on things. When I woke up and tried to comfort her, she would eventually calm down but as soon as I fell asleep she would wake me up acting crazy again. I was feeling guilty about getting the cat and realized at the same time that this solution was not going to let me get any sleep anyway. I was just about at my wit's end...

The following morning, I woke up and realized that I did not hear the cat. I feared that she might be dead and I looked all over the place for her. I found her curled up in a ball in my bedroom (that I never used) on the floor in the corner, somewhat hidden under the comforter. She was not dead, just sleeping. I thought maybe she just had a restless night, being in a different place and hoped that tonight we could both get some sleep. That did not happen, same thing all over again. The cat was acting crazy, waking me up all hours of the night. The next day I took the cat back to the shelter and told them that I didn't think it was going to be a good match, and they took her back. At least I did not have to have it on my conscience that the cat died because I used her to keep the spirit away. I can say that I did not have any bad dreams while the cat was there, but I did not get much sleep either.

I really think the cat did some good, or maybe it was the salt water. It was probably a combination of all of that and the fact that I talked to the spirit and told it I was moving and to please leave me alone. I also prayed and read my Bible every night, which I had been doing since all of this first started.

I prepared the mixture of herbs and explained to the landlord what I was doing because he was going to see these garlic cloves on the floor in the living room and a trail of herbs going out the door to the parking area. He just laughed at me. I know he thinks I am a nutcase. Anyway, after two months of practically no sleep, I was finally moving out. Casper did not follow me, I hope the cat lived and most people that I tell this story to think I am crazy. Except for the few who have once had a Casper in their lives.

ALASKA

AS TOLD BY: CHAD DEES

When I was young we lived in a trailer at the back of a trailer park. It is called the Diamond Estates and it is in Anchorage, Alaska, off of Dimond and Arctic. In this place the woods were my backyard and I spent the majority of my time there. But when I wasn't out there I spent a lot of time reading in my room or laying on the couch with my book, discovering worlds of fantasy or science fiction. I loved Tolkien, Brian Jacques, and many others. Sometimes though, reality was just as strange as the books I read.

When my stepfather moved in with us, which was only a few days after we moved into the trailer ourselves, he told us all almost immediately of strange dreams he was having involving most of the members of our family being possessed and he being subject to their demonic rage and torment. He even experienced dreams of himself being possessed over time. The only person he never talked about being possessed in these nightmares was me. He would wake up each morning with some new tale of horror and fear to tell us all at breakfast. None of the stories in his dreams ever made me suspect anything until I was much older. This went on for several years.

One Friday evening my mom and stepdad had gone out for the night and I was watching my brother and sister for them. The evening was uneventful for the majority of it. My siblings were surprisingly well behaved and they went to bed fairly easily. I laid on the couch watching TV without really paying much attention to it. I was mostly daydreaming about the adventures awaiting my friends and I in the woods the next day. I couldn't wait for the weekend to be in full swing. Most Saturday mornings we would sleep in a little late and then spend all day in the woods battling monsters and each other, building forts and traps, or playing jokes on each other.

I suddenly was struck with a sensation that I was not really familiar with at that point in my life but would later become fully acquainted with. The feeling of the hair on the back of my neck and arms standing up, my skin felt like ants were crawling on it, and my stomach giving a subtle tingle; the feeling was strong and a little scary. Someone was watching me surreptitiously. My eyes sought out the source of the feeling and at first saw nothing but were pulled up to a spot near the ceiling and just along the edge of the wall dividing our living room and our kitchen.

There was someone standing there with their hand gripping the wall and their face aimed at me. They were watching me. As I felt my eyes make contact with theirs, the head and hand disappeared back around the corner and I heard what sounded like a huge man, go running down the hall. Down the hall towards the rooms with my sleeping siblings in them, I could not let them be hurt. I grabbed my baseball bat and ran towards the hall. As I neared the long dark hallway, I became cautious realizing that to rush into danger might mean I would be incapable of offering any real aid to my brother and sister.

I paused and listened and heard nothing. The house was still and silent and dark. I felt a stronger stirring in my gut. I was afraid but I would not abandon my siblings to their fate. I flicked the light switch and gloried in the application of light to the long dark hallway. My fear lessened but was still there. This stranger could hurt me and probably easily. I was a large child but still a child.

I walked down the hallway past my brother's room since the pounding steps sounded like they had gone all the way to the end of the hallway to my sister's room. The door was closed, the house was still quiet and seemingly calm. I feared the shattering of that calm with violence. I feared for my life and those of my brother and sister. I could not allow them to be hurt however so I turned the knob and stepped into my sister's dark room.

Her room was simple and sparse. She had a bed, desk, night stand and closet in her room. She lay sleeping in her bed soundly. She was utterly undisturbed. Her closet had no doors and contained almost nothing. She had a few dresses hanging and some shirts. I could see the back of her shallow closet from a few steps inside the door. I flipped the light on anyway and she muttered in her sleep, but didn't move or wake. I walked over to her closet and shoved the clothes to one side. I saw nothing but newly painted wall.

I walked over to her window and looked at it, it was unbroken, closed and locked. It was completely secure. I looked around the whole room and saw everything completely normal and totally undisturbed. I began to think something was strange but was still mostly in defensive mode. I hadn't formed the questions but had the inkling of doubts forming in my head. I left the room and turned off the light.

I walked back up the hall to my parent's room and tried to turn the knob. It was locked and the door didn't budge. The doubts were still circling but not coalescing just yet.

The next door up was mine and my brother's and I fully expected to find an intruder in there. I felt the knob and listened at the door. All seemed quiet and normal beyond the door. I heard no sound on the other side, certainly nothing frightening or dangerous. I turned the knob and shoved the door open. My brother lay sleeping in his bed and no one jumped out and grabbed me.

I looked around the room and saw nothing untoward. My carefully arranged figurines were still carefully arranged. My desk was closed as were our closet doors. My eyes locked on the closet doors, I clutched the bat tighter and choked up a little and walked towards the closet. Then I went back and turned on the light. My brother didn't even stir when the lights came on. He slept on peacefully, blissfully unaware of the intruder. I looked at him with a fondness I didn't always show when he was awake.

I eased closer to the closet and centered myself carefully. I placed my feet carefully to have maximum balance if I had to swing. I managed my breathing and stifled my fear as much as I could. I stepped closer and placed my hand on the closet door feeling for the slightest trembling. Was his hand pressed to the other side of the door even then? I felt nothing and still heard nothing. I flung the door open.

Inside I saw all my brother's jackets hanging with huge gaps between them. I could see the wall and the floor underneath them. There was no one hiding on this end. I walked to my side and flung it open as well and no one leaped out and attacked me. I saw my jackets hanging neatly and my woods gear and my piles of magazines. I saw no intruder.

I walked to our window and saw that it was just as secure as my sister's had been. It was closed, locked and unmolested. I looked around the room again and saw nothing disturbed. No one had been in here but my brother and I all day. I ran from the room and checked all the windows and doors in the house again. The doubts and questions leapt to life in my brain with a feeling like being zapped with an electrical discharge. Someone had invaded our house and disappeared.

Something unexplainable had been in our house and it terrified me. I woke my brother and sister up and made sure they weren't playing a prank, but I could tell by how difficult they were to wake that it hadn't been either of them. They were both innocent and confused. They went back to sleep. I sat on the couch and waited for my parents to come home and clutched my bat like a talisman. I cried a lot as I contemplated possibilities.

When my parents finally arrived they didn't believe me. They ridiculed me and said I had been dreaming. They laughed it off. In time, I got past the fear but I never forgot. My stepfather's nightmares continued.

A few months later, he woke up one morning and said that the dreams hadn't come the night before. He had slept through the night and felt wonderfully rested. That night my sister had a friend spend the night and the next morning he again didn't have any nightmares of demonic possession. He slept fantastically again. He dreamt of regular things like flying and falling.

After lunch, my sister's friend went into the bathroom while we were all still sitting at the table. I heard her turn the light on and then a pause and a terror filled scream erupted from her little throat. She came scrambling backwards out of the bathroom. Her eyes were huge and all the blood had left her face and extremities. She was babbling and her eyes were rolling in their sockets. Her hands were wound up in the front of her shirt rooting like two little rats.

My parents gathered around her and tried to calm her down. She slowly eased back from the edge of full-on terrified panic. I walked into the bathroom and looked around. I saw nothing out of place. I sat on the edge of the tub and ran my hands along the inside, it was completely dry. As I walked out of the bathroom I heard her say that there had been a girl in the bathroom.

She was still jittery and her eyes were still huge and staring but she was calm enough to describe what she'd seen. A girl who appeared to be between 4 and 7 years old had been laying in the tub, covered with water and had reached out and tried to touch her. The girl had been wearing an elaborate yellow dress and her hair had been done up as if for a ball. She had screamed and backed out of the bathroom. When I went back into the bathroom the tub was still dry. My stepfather never had another dream of someone being possessed the whole rest of the time that we lived in that trailer.

Of course this was merely the beginning of some of the many supernatural or paranormal things that I have seen or felt or been touched by. I have seen much and felt more growing up and living in Anchorage, Alaska.

ARIZONA

As told by: Marissa Marie

I had always been a bit sensitive to the paranormal. My family has known this but they refuse to believe me when I tell them about John. John is the name that I have given to one of our friendly house ghosts. My family likes to ignore his existence merely because they are terrified of the idea that there is someone in the house that they cannot see. I, myself, cannot see John, but I know he is here. I know by paying attention to my surroundings and by the small, strange occurrences that happen every so often.

I noticed that John was present when doors started to open and close on their own. It's mainly my bedroom door. I have attempted to debunk this as evidence by putting a door stop in front of it. I wanted to make sure that it wasn't caused by the air-conditioner or other doors opening and closing. It would still open and close by itself.

John also likes to turn TVs on and off. He knows how to change the stations on Pandora if he doesn't like the music that is playing. These are all subtle occurrences that happen from time to time.

There are other things that happen that I choose to acknowledge.

Every now and then, footsteps can be heard going up and down the hallway while everyone else is sound asleep. I have gotten up and checked many times to make sure that it isn't my family.

Sometimes, a disembodied voice can be heard. It is the voice of a male. He will whisper several different phrases and words. Some are: "hello", "thank you", "wait", "come here", "Cindy", "mom" and "Marissa". I enjoy the fact that he has learned my name.

One night, I was very tired and I didn't feel like getting up to turn off the light.

So I jokingly said, "Please turn off the light for me, John. I'm too tired to get up right now."

Amazingly, I saw the light switch start to go down and the light shut off. I think that this would scare most people. I found it spectacular that I was able to interact with the paranormal. I told John thank you before I went to sleep.

It seems that the more I mention or try to communicate with John, the more active he becomes. He is also learning to do more things. He recently learned how to touch people.

I realized this when I was lying down and watching something on Netflix. I felt someone place a hand on my upper back. I turned around and expected to see my mom standing there. No one was to be seen. I shrugged it off and continued to watch Netflix. This has happened a few more times since then. I don't mind it.

I have tried to convince my family to let me conduct a small paranormal investigation. They have refused to let me go forward with one. My mother says that it would be "inviting evil into the house". I hope they will agree to one someday.

That's all I have to tell you about John. I will be keeping an eye out for any other kind of activity that may show up. I can't wait to see what happens in the future.

ARKANSAS

AS TOLD BY: KATHY BOLTON

A little over a decade ago, my kids and I moved to Arkansas and quickly found ourselves to be on the verge of homelessness. Miraculously, I stumbled across an abandoned house. Long story short, I found the owner of the home and received permission for my children and I to move in. Several people told me stories of ghosts in this home but a haunted home does not bother me so we promptly moved in. We lived there for over a month before I could have a hot water heater put in and hook up running water to the home.

This was a rather dark period in my life and to say that I was more or less dropping the ball is almost an understatement. I was depressed and not attending to my household as I should have; often the home was quite messy and unkempt. I noticed that when I did not keep up the home weird things happened.

One night during a thunderstorm, our landline phone literally blew up and flew across the room in pieces. We thought lightning had hit the line and traveled into the house but nothing else was affected; the television and the computer were both on at the time. Looking back, I wonder how only the phone was affected. New light bulbs would often blow out, dishes would somehow fall off of the countertops and break even though no one was in the kitchen and it didn't take more than two months before the brand new water heater inexplicably broke.

Somehow I sensed that this was all due to the displeasure of the ghosts we could feel (and sometimes hear) at my lax housekeeping habits. When I began to keep the house up again the entire atmosphere of the home lightened somehow.

This went on for about three or four months however, due to the ups and downs of divorce and relocating over 700 miles from my home and family, when my kids left to visit their father for the summer I slumped back into depression and ignored my housekeeping once again.

As soon as the house became a mess, the second new water heater simply died and several pipes burst. Having to spend the money to repair them snapped me back to reality and I straightened up.

I could feel the difference in the atmosphere of the house once again. I began to talk to the entities I could feel in the home; I thought there was a woman there.

One day I was in the kitchen doing the dishes and I caught something moving out of the corner of my eye. I turned my head to see what had caught my attention somewhat behind and to the right of me. Walking from the bathroom, through the back of the kitchen and toward the living room was the full body apparition of a man dressed in a three-piece gray flannel or wool suit, with a white shirt, dark tie, and he was wearing an old fashioned gray hat with a black hat band. His shoes were dark and of a similar style to old fashioned men's dress shoes. He was rather stern looking and was tall and thin with short dark hair. The style of clothing was perhaps from the 1930s or '40s.

He did not look at me nor acknowledge me in any way. I could clearly see a somber expression on his face; I watched him take two or three steps before he simply vanished into thin air before my eyes.

The wall behind him was different somehow and it was like the items I had against that wall were suddenly not there; he was walking right through a large bird cage but where he stood the cage did not exist. It is difficult to describe the difference in the wall and items as the apparition only lasted a very short time and I was focused on the man himself rather than the difference in surroundings. It was quite startling and very clear but only for about 30 seconds or so. It was the middle of the day and the kitchen was bright and sunny. I remember thinking that it was far too hot out for anyone to be dressed in such a suit. I did not feel scared by this presence but I felt as though he was in some way letting me see him to tell me that he expected, and insisted upon the home being kept in a tidy condition.

Although I continued to hear things and items seemed to move in the home when the kids swore they hadn't touched anything, if I left any type of a mess when I went to bed or work, I never saw anyone again. If I left a sink load of dirty dishes overnight often I would awaken to something broken on the kitchen floor in the morning, even when I was the only person in the home that night.

Whenever the man I was dating would spend the night things would happen; it was almost like they disapproved of a single mother in general but really disapproved of a single mother dating intimately. Often things on the kitchen or bathroom selves would be on the floor in the morning.

I believe that an older couple from a more traditional time occupied the home and they would quickly express their disapproval whenever I did not act in a traditional way. I do not think they approved of me but always had the impression and the feeling that they cared for the children. Nothing belonging to my children was ever moved or broken.

I tried to discover who this man could have been but never did figure it out and I could never discover if anyone had died in the home or on the property. I never saw a woman; that is simply something I felt and the feeling I had was that she was not as harsh or disapproving as the man was.

While I did have pet dogs at the time I did not have a cat and many of the items that had somehow gone from a shelf to the floor could not have been reached by the dogs. In case you're wondering, I have no history of mental illness, was not taking drugs either illegal or prescription, nor have I ever experienced hallucinations; I have, however, always been somewhat sensitive to many aspects of the paranormal.

CALIFORNIA

AS TOLD BY: SIMONA HARPER

I am 33 years old and I look back at my childhood and remember the day that scared me so bad, I will never forget.

I was 12 years old and I lived in Ben Lomond, California at the time. My mother did warehouse work and my father was a computer engineer. It was around 8:30 in the morning and I planned on riding my bike to school instead of walking. We lived close to the school up in the mountains so I was able to get there alone.

Humming along while riding my bike, I passed a car that was abandoned. I didn't think anything of it at the time because I was focused on getting to school, though it crossed my mind what if... I slowed down to look inside and I saw my cat with its head missing laying on the front seat. I started screaming for help as I was so terrified I didn't know what to do.

So I got on my bike and pedaled back home in a panic. I called my mother at work to tell her what I had seen. She told me to stay home and wait for her. So I was waiting and panicking and crying uncontrollably. I went outside and looked down the driveway to see if my mom was pulling in. I blinked my eyes for a second and I saw my cat on the porch walking towards me, I screamed with confusion and fear. I picked Yodi up and she was totally fine. I thought to myself, what did I see on my way to school? My mother arrived in a panic in total fear for my life. I explained what happened and she said I was just imagining things. I said I am telling the truth let me take you there and show you what I saw. We got in the car and drove to the place where I saw the car parked. It was a white Cadillac that had been abandoned.

The car was still there. My mother walked up to the car and saw a woman lying in the front seat. I don't know what happened to her but I assumed it was terrible because my mother was screaming and running towards me to get out of there! When she got in the car her face was as white as a ghost and she could hardly talk. I was crying and asking her what she saw. I had to tell her to slow down as she was hauling ass to go get help. We arrived at the police station to make a report of our sighting. We were told to stay there. They dispatched the ambulance and the police were on their way I guess... It all happened so fast.

When they arrived to the place where we saw the car, there was nothing there.

What did we see? Where did it go? I know it wasn't a dream! I will never forget that day and I know now it was paranormal. It had to have been. The memory is so fresh in my mind to this day, it still freaks me out and my mother pretends nothing ever happened...

COLORADO

AS TOLD BY: AMY MATTISON

I had lived in my Denver, Colorado basement two-bedroom apartment for over a year when I met my current husband. I had two small children at the time, ages 3 and 5. There had been no negative energy in our home up until he moved in with us. Upon his arrival I purchased an antique dresser from a local dealer. I remember taking notice of the discounted price I paid for it from the original price offered. It was a local dealer and I figured it was a piece they had for some time that they were trying to get out of their inventory.

Little did I know that the moment the dresser set foot in my home the air thickened and the encounters began. It started with my children having nightmares. Not your normal scary dreams but screaming-out-in-the-middle-of-the-night inconsolable nightmares. Along with the nightmares came our family cat, Ruka, not setting foot in either of the two bedrooms ever. This is a kitty that slept with one family member or another, under the covers any day of the week. These simple changes went unnoticed for a couple months until the air thickened and things happening were impossible to ignore.

The children continued to experience nightmares and the cat grew distant from family life. Before long the doorbell would ring at random and alarm clocks would reset as if we'd lost power. I could no longer set my alarm for work. It so happened that my then position required me to awake during the 3 a.m. hour. I would set my alarm clock for 3:30 daily and it would consistently fail. Blinking as if power had been disconnected yet the rest of the clocks in the house were fine. The air was cold and there was a sense of fear around. Televisions would turn on at random and the doorbell would ring as it pleased.

One night I went to bed before my husband and I experienced a night I would never forget. My husband tucked me into bed saying he was leaving for the gym. I began to nod off when my bed started shaking uncontrollably. It was below the bed furiously shaking the entire mattress. I recall saying a prayer to protect myself and the children and ignoring the terror that pulsed through my veins. My husband came and kissed me upon his arrival from the gym and I asked him if he had been shaking my bed and he said he hadn't been home for the last two hours. I can still feel the fierceness the mattress shook with to this day.

Immediately after the bed shaking encounter, I blessed the home stating, "you are not welcome here; please do not enter my home" with salt and sage. It seemed to work keeping whatever may be outside the home. I say that because it seemed to taunt us every time we'd come home by ringing the doorbell every time we crossed the threshold.

My children reported seeing a woman around the house that I never encountered but all came to an end after moving to a new home. We still have the dresser that I originally blamed the interaction with, but to this day simply wonder if our old location simply did not agree with our new house mate or my current husband.

CONNECTICUT

AS TOLD BY: Kristianne Hall

The record played through the living room and the kitchen while we made dinner just low enough for conversation and jabbing remarks. The flow of voices and music was easy and relaxed. People moved throughout the rooms uninterrupted. I found the figure in the back hallway when I opened the doorway. It glowed orange and yellow, with a golden collar of light. Although difficult to see its obstructed face, I saw it was a young girl.

I took a step forward and she receded into the back wall and faded into the beam of light permanently on the old wooden floor.

I wasn't afraid, but I was guarded and conflicted. I considered it for a minute there in the hallway. I looked into the mirror in the bathroom to reassure myself that I could see clearly. I cleaned my glasses quickly and washed my hands out of habit. But when I went back to the kitchen I didn't see anybody, as if there would be no one to listen to me if I spoke. The sauce and water bubbled menacingly.

To face the figure was a challenging psychological defeat. I wondered if I should speak over the music loudly and abrasively, or if when the side was over I could softly remark on my observation. The living room was jovial, and the cats were excitedly jumping over the couches and onto the tables to the delight of the guests. Jacob became placid and quiet suddenly, and he asked me if I was going to say anything. It was his apartment, and he obviously already knew. We exchanged some worried looks. I stuttered for a minute as I asked for a beer. He granted my wish with a Miller High and sat next to me.

What I really wanted was to see it again, so I could understand what its purpose was. He told me she was protecting him, and that her collar of gold was meant to explain her inability to communicate. What was she protecting him from? Was it safe to open us up to such psychic and telekinetic interference?

I discovered that the others had quieted and began watching our nervous motions. The table abruptly stopped turning and the record stopped, the sounds of cars driving by flowed through the window freely. Dave asked who died and why we weren't flipping the record. I told him it was okay to play something I just didn't feel like doing it. Jacob got up to do it and stopped, he told me he wanted to talk. I agreed, but was uneasy about the content of the conversation.

I asked what he meant by "protective" as in, "what are the other features of his apartment that may be in need of protection." My room was downstairs two floors and I only felt and imagined things, I never physically saw or observed any type of paranormal or supernatural movement. What I had seen in the hallway was more than I had ever experienced in the past. He began stringing a prism in the overpass of the door, and showed me where the other one was located in the doorway of his bedroom about twelve paces away.

"If I found the source in the house I would be able to do something about it. But as of right now it's just a solemn and terrifying figure that lurks in doorways and hallways, and shuts them after a cold wind blows through it."

Jacob seemed relieved to share all of it, but I wondered why he hadn't said anything before. I began to wonder if I was the cause of the negative energy, if I was somehow bringing in the worst of the worst just by being there. No one else seemed to experience this guilt or wild imagination of ghosts.

The moment she came to the table, I didn't feel fearful. The energy when she walked up was different. I could move my body a little more and I felt a strange trust for her. I knew she wasn't going to harm me.

Oddly, she was very attractive. She had long white hair that covered the slightest hint of breasts. She had the most beautiful ultramarine violet eyes.

She didn't have a nose but she had plump lips. She had an hourglass figure and a very peaceful demeanor.

I remember vividly her climbing on top of me. I knew her intention was to have sex with me. This is a little embarrassing to admit but I was instantly ready to go. I felt a bit nervous, yet peaceful as she climbed on top of me. She said nothing as she placed my part inside of her.

The minute I was inside it felt amazing. I've been with my fair share of women and this was like nothing I had ever felt before. The three little aliens watched us as she rode me. We didn't kiss, or talk. It was a very clinical sexual encounter. A scientist doing research.

Within a couple of minutes I felt like I was about to blow. My breathing changed and I let out the most explosive orgasm I had ever had. I must have released all of the sperm inside of me; and she immediately climbed off of me after my climax.

The intensity of the orgasm put me to sleep almost immediately. I don't remember anyone saying or doing anything. All I remember is falling to sleep heavily.

I had never cheated on my wife before. I had never cheated period. And although I want to say an alien sexually assaulted me, I kind of wanted her to.

Maybe it was brainpower over mine, but the minute I saw her I wanted to be seduced.

The next thing I remember I was back in my car. The car was on and running fine. The clock said it was 2:20 a.m. and I couldn't believe my eyes. I had been gone for hours. My wife was worried sick when I came in and I told her how sorry I was, and when I tried to tell her what happened she wanted no part of it. No excuses. There was nothing more I could do but tell her what seemed to be an unbelievable truth. What else had they done to me while I was in their presence? I have so many questions about that night that I'm sure will never be answered.

DELAWARE

AS TOLD BY: ELAINE LEVADITIS

Marie was born the 15th of 16 children to poor Polish immigrant farmers. Many days while the family toiled in the fields, Marie was placed in an old wooden playpen, much to her discontent. Bored with the entire situation, Marie had a habit of jumping in the playpen for attention which lovingly earned her the nickname, "Frog". Marie led a fairly difficult life, marrying then divorcing a musician, whose union resulted in me, then marrying a military man whose experience in Vietnam and the chemical Agent Orange produced three mentally challenged children. Marie and her second husband Harold were heavy smokers, but after 20 years they both were finally able to quit, most likely due to the severity of their daughter's asthma. Still the damage was already done, and Marie developed a cancerous spot on her left lung, and was given a grim diagnosis: one year at the most. As I lived on the other side of the country, visiting was difficult and costly, but when I got word that her condition had taken a turn for the worse, I booked a flight out to the Midwest. I had always been terrified of planes, but now there was no time to drive. While on the plane I tried to keep occupied with the magazine I had brought, but my mind was racing between fear of the flight, and fear of what I might find when I got to my mother's side. I looked out the window staring into the clouds and praying when appeared the most perfect rainbow circle. Inside the circle was the entire shadow of the plane. It only lasted for a few seconds, and I looked down at my watch to see how much longer I had to endure the flight and the time was 7:21.

At the airport I was met by my sister and stepfather. Too late. I had missed saying goodbye to my mother by less than an hour. Marie took her last breath and was pronounced dead at...7:21. The next few days were hectic. My stepfather asked us to remove our mother's things, and to divide them amongst ourselves. After saying goodbye to my mom "the Frog", I was exhausted and anxious to get back home to my old routine. After what seemed an excruciatingly long drive home from the airport, I was happy to see my house from down the road. As I approached, something was blocking my access to my driveway. I stepped out of my vehicle to discover a frog, nearly the size of a dinner plate sitting calmly in the road! A frog of that size is unheard of in coastal Delaware, and it took two hands to pick it up but I put it in my car and set it free in the nearby wooded area.

Over the next couple of years Harold began to date, and found a woman who filled the void in his lonely life, and he married her. Soon after she moved in, she began to take many falls on the basement stairs, claiming she was "pushed". My sister began reporting to me that my mother would come to her, dressed in her pink nightgown. She would sit on the foot of my sister's bed. My sister said she also heard a lot of scary noises, doors slamming and voices. I told her I did not think that the Frog was responsible for that, but the noises frightened her, and she had her house blessed by a priest and holy water. Soon after, she said the noises stopped, but regrettably, the visits did too. Harold and his wife decided that since this was effective, they should do the same, and it was successful, there were no more stair accidents afterward.

The following Christmas, the family was to get together in Arkansas. I drove down ahead, and Harold and his new wife were to arrive the next day. They packed up the car with Christmas gifts. It was a beautiful Lincoln Continental, my mother's dream car that she had saved for over 10 years to buy. Although the weather was perfect for December, Harold lost control of the vehicle. He claimed he hydroplaned across four lanes of traffic into the oncoming traffic, although there had not been any precipitation for several days prior. The car was struck by a semi-truck and thrown several hundred feet into the ditch. The entire passenger side of the car was destroyed, and Harold's wife a twisted mass of flesh and bones, but still barely alive. Harold emerged from the vehicle without so much as a scratch or bruise, but badly shaken up. I jumped in my car and drove back to the accident with Harold, as Christmas gifts were scattered over a large area of highway, and in his shock seemed overly concerned about "cleaning up the mess" as he put it. "This ones for you" he said, picking up a gift barely still wrapped. "It was your moms, and I know she would have wanted you to have it". As I tore off the rest of the paper, I was amazed at how this fragile porcelain figure survived such an accident without any damage.

Yes, Harold's wife did survive, although Harold only lived a few months longer. She will most likely be in pain for the rest of her life, but also suffered some brain damage. And I did find out why someone as sweet as The Frog would go to such extremes. You see Harold's greedy new wife wanted everything, including my handicapped sister's trust fund, and threatened Harold to leave everything to her. Once she was physically unable to care for my sister as a guardian, it was easy for me to petition for guardianship and challenge the will. My mother was finally able to rest, knowing that I would be here to take care of my sisters, just as I had promised her, while frightened and tearful, looking out a plane window at 7:21.

FLORIDA

AS TOLD BY: Daniel Pojoga

When I was 9 years old, I lived in Hollywood, Florida. I was outside sitting in the middle of the courtyard of the apartment complex. When in the distance, I saw something jumping very high and fast from roof to roof. It had jumped into the tree behind the apartment complex. I went to look around the apartment at the tree. Whatever it was, it jumped down onto our apartment complex. It was looking right at me. It was a 7 feet tall, 3 feet wide Rottweiler mixed with bulldog with an enormous head. As it looked at me, it started to change shape, into an oblong looking person. With a tall head, very skinny body, crimson eyes, and exhaling what looked like exhaust. Before I knew it, my legs were moving and I was running towards the door. The second I look back, it lunges from the roof and on top of me, back in its vicious looking dog form. It was on top of me, the weight of it felt like a 3 ton truck. Sniffing, it gave one loud thunderous snarl, and jumped off. I was paralyzed there for a moment, not due to fear, but I can't say what.

Those glowing red eyes had once shown themselves before. When I lived in my other house in Hollywood. I fell asleep on the couch with my father, and woke up around 3-4a.m. When I opened my eyes, those eyes were staring right at me. Thinking it was the television, I turned it on, only to illuminate its body, I shut the television off. But before the light extinguished, it was in front of my face glaring at me. I shut my eyes, and hid under the blanket while I was trying to wake up my father. But he never woke up, not until after it disappeared into the darkness.

The last time I saw it, I was living in Boca Raton, Florida. It was the second week in October, when I was at a park with some friends late at night. The air was thick with fog and a sense of gravity. When the time hit 11:37, my friends said that I just stopped. I stood there looking into the distance with my mouth agape. When I came too, they were trying to fill me in, on the way I was behaving. But I wasn't able to take my focus off of the portal-like hole that was growing bigger in the distance. What came out of it, was that tremendous Bull-rot, as I call it. The difference this time, was that it was on a chain and the chain continued to flow through the hole. The air got thicker and colder. My friends even noticed that. When I told them we should probably go, they almost agreed. Then as soon as we decided we should go, I looked around us. We were surrounded by spectral beings of shapes and sizes that didn't make sense. Most did not have a full body. Some were just split in two, hanging together by only a little flesh. I look back towards the "hole in the universe" and see that an enormous figure is stepping through. The chain clenched in its massive, blackened hands. When it stepped through, it was like the sky knew to get extremely dark, clouds rolled in over the moon. We were being closed in upon, by hundreds of beings that should not be here. I started for a run towards the car, which was only 30 feet away. When I did, the others joined in, and before I knew it we were driving away, being chased down by that damned dog and its master.

After driving for what felt like 30 minutes, but was more like 30 seconds, they disappeared. And the moon came out, the fog went away, and we all felt better. After we all pulled over to puke.

GEORGIA

AS TOLD BY: Tristan Hart

When I was in high school, I and a few friends were very interested in the paranormal, but we sought to enter that world ourselves rather than seeking ghosts and haunted places in this world. My friend (we'll call him Todd) had a book entitled "*The Projection of the Astral Body*", and it detailed an early 20th century account of a young man who experimented with Astral Projection and out-of-body experiences. He discussed that those who were sicklier, were prone to escape their bodies more readily, as he was, and that he was able to manifest sounds and even sometimes interact with light objects when he was in the Astral State.

Todd had read and studied the book for far longer than I or our other friend (we'll call him Mike), and so he was further along with its studies and had even attempted an out-of-body experience a time or two. Mike and I were just getting into it when the three of us took a trip out to the local lake on a Friday night after school.

Todd began by sitting calmly in a chair and studying the horizon. We were just kids, hanging out with nothing to do, so we all attempted what the book told us. Todd was the only one that was successful.

Afterward, he told me that he had seen a light on the far side of the lake, and he had slowly floated toward it until it engulfed his vision. Afterward, he spoke of being a bit confused, and of seeing himself from above, that sort of thing.

Now, all of this could be chalked up to young minds wanting to believe something, but what happened next was cold, hard fact, and I'm still unsure how it could be.

We began to worry about Todd, and whether he was okay, so Mike put his hand on Todd's chest to check his heart and breathing. After a few moments he murmured, "That's strange..."

"What?" I asked.

"His breathing is matching mine," Mike replied.

I made a disgusted face as I worked out what that meant. "Let me see," I said to him, full of skepticism.

I sat at arm's length, with nothing but my hand touching Todd's chest. I steadied my breathing for a bit before I noticed that he was, indeed, matching mine. That could be coincidence, so I tried a test. I started to inhale slowly, so as to hold my breath. Keep in mind that Todd is passed out and not touching me in any way at this point.

His chest started to expand slowly, as well. The moment I stopped, so did his. I counted to 23 while I held my breath, picking an odd number, just to see what would happen. The moment I thought the number '24' and let my breath out, Todd did the exact same.

I'm still at a loss for how a kid who was unconscious and not touching me could sync his breathing with mine, and I may hesitate to call it very paranormal, but it is definitely something I still grasp at straws to explain at 30 years old.

HAWAI'I

As told by: Anonymous

I had purchased a house from a man who was going to be moving in with one of his sons as he was getting on in years and needed a little more help with day-to-day things. He had raised his family in the home and lived there for many years so the transition was hard for him. We reached an agreement that, although I would be able to move in at closing, he would have some things still in the garage and basement and would have help from family members to get all of his belongings out within a week or two. On the day that I was moving in, he was at the house and told me that he had somehow misplaced one of his favorite smoking pipes. He thought that he had laid it down on the kitchen counter but couldn't find it anywhere. It seemed to be quite upsetting to him although he had many more, so I promised that I would look for it and if I found it, would let him know right away. And since he was going to be coming over during the following couple of weeks to collect the rest of his belongings, I would set it aside so that he could pick it up.

I had a few friends help me move the things from my small apartment into my new home and had offered to compensate them with pizza and beer.

After everything was moved in, and dinner was finished, everyone began to file out wishing me well on my first night in my new house. As the last person was getting ready to leave, I asked him if he could please go in and replace the toilet seat with the new one that I had purchased. I had already put a new black seat cover and rug into the bathroom and wanted a new toilet seat to make it feel more fresh and mine. He went into the bathroom while I cleaned up the pizza boxes and the rest of the dinner mess. I had just finished when he came out. I thanked him and let him know that it was just in time because I had to relieve myself of the liquid refreshments from the day. I walked into the bathroom and found a driver's license lying face down on top of the bathroom rug. I assumed that it belonged to my friend that had been on his knees installing my toilet seat, and that maybe it came out of his pocket while he was bent over. Without looking at it, I set it on the edge of the sink, did what I had come in there to do, washed and dried my hands and then looked at the license. It belonged to a female who had the same last name as the man that I had just bought the house from.

I came out of the bathroom and asked my friend where he had found the driver's license. He looked a little confused and asked, "What license?" I replied, "The license that was lying on top of the bathroom rug. You had to see it. The rug is black so anything that's not black, like a white driver's license, would stand out." He again denied seeing anything in the bathroom, even when I showed it to him. I set it on top of a shelf near the front door, assuming that it must belong to one of the former owner's relatives and maybe they had dropped it and somehow or another, maybe it got stuck to the bottom of my friend's boot and just happened to come off as he left my bathroom. Whatever had happened, I would make sure to return it to the family the next day when they came over to retrieve another load of belongings.

When the former owner showed up the next day, I greeted him at the door and chatted with him for a few minutes. He was about to walk down the steps to go to the garage when I remembered the license. I stopped him and explained that one of his family members must have dropped their license as they were helping him move the day before. He took it from me, looked at it and had tears well up in his eyes. I noticed that his hand began to shake and he looked towards the driveway where one of his kids was waiting for him. His son came towards him and asked, "Dad, what's wrong?" He just handed the license to his son. The son looked at it and then up at me and asked, "Where did you get this?" I explained to him what happened the night before. He then turned back towards his dad who was now down in the drive wiping his eyes. He said, "Dad, I thought you had put all of her stuff away." His father replied, "I did. We put everything in a box and I have never opened it." The son then explained to me that the license belonged to his sister who had died many years previous in a terrible accident.

I had many other things happen in that house over the years that I lived there. Everything from hearing footsteps like someone was walking in heels on a hardwood floor even though I had installed carpet in most every room, to hearing someone knock very loudly on my front door even though the motion sensor light was never activated and the screen door was locked so it could not have come from outside the house.

IDAHO

AS TOLD BY: STACEY SPINTS

One instance that I had that I believe was due to the paranormal happened one day when my mom and I were sitting in the living room watching television, and we suddenly heard a crash come from the front bathroom. There was a candle holder that had sand and seashells in it that was originally sitting on the back part of the toilet and it had somehow fallen off of that and broke. We were both kind of puzzled by that because it sat right in the center, not close to the edge at all.

When my sister was two years old, she had a lot of toys that played music or talked when you pushed buttons or squeezed the toy. She had this one toy out in the living room with her among other toys. It was a stuffed dog that you could squeeze the ear, the tummy, the paw, et cetera and it would talk. It was sitting in the big La-Z-Boy chair across from me. My sister wasn't playing with it and my mom was sitting right next to me the whole time. The toy suddenly screams out "I LOVE YOU!" I thought that was very odd and creepy, so I either switched off the toy or took out the batteries.

Another instance that really creeped me out happened very late at night. I am the night owl of the family and like staying up late. This happened around 3:00 a.m. I was sitting on my bed doing something on my laptop, when I suddenly heard a bubbling noise coming from my sister's room which is right next to mine. I opened my door and listened. I soon realized that it was coming from my sister's little play kitchen. There's a little stove burner that makes a bubbling noise like you're cooking something or boiling some water whenever you put one of the play pans on it. The noise went on for a really long time and when it stopped I went into her room to investigate. I looked at the burner and put my hand on it to see if that would trigger the noise, but it didn't. Upon closer inspection, there was a button in the grooves that could only be triggered by matching grooves in the play pans and is actually very difficult to press with your own finger. This fact made me a bit worried and gave me a "this is very weird" feeling. So I went back into my room and once I was back in my room, the bubbling noise started again, but it was much louder this time, and the noise seemed to go on forever.

Later on, I ended up moving in with my grandparents for a while because of some issues at home. Sometimes my mom would tell me that my sister's toys would go off by themselves, but that was the only thing that happened AT HOME after I left. Whatever it was that kept messing with my sister's toys must have followed me to my grandparents at one point. When I moved in with my grandparents, I had to stay in the kid's room, which had some toys in it like what my sister had at home, but only one toy made any noise. It was a toy turtle that had shapes on the shell that would play music when pressed and played music when it was pulled across the room. There were a number of nights where I woke up in the middle of the night to that turtle playing music. After a couple of nights of it doing that, I finally said "that's enough," and put the turtle in the living room. It stopped going off after that.

Whatever it was stopped making the toys go off, too. Haven't had any more experiences since what happened with the turtle.

ILLINOIS

AS TOLD BY: Dorraine Fisher

You think you know what's real in this world until something happens to shake up your paradigms.

Some years ago, I lived in an old Victorian house near our downtown area. I loved the house because it was huge and roomy and had a lot of character. But it was well over a hundred years old; creaky and squeaky and settling like it had a life of its own. And it wouldn't be long before I found out how true that statement was.

One day, as I was watching TV in the living room, I heard strange noises that seemed to come from upstairs. My roommate traveled for her job and was gone a lot, but when she was home, I could often hear her upstairs walking around in the hallway. But on this particular day, she wasn't home.

I muted the TV volume to listen more closely, and I heard what sounded like her up there walking around.

There was a spot in the floor that squeaked in a particular way any time someone stepped over it.

And that's what it was. I'd heard it so many times from downstairs.

The dog had noticed it first and stood at the foot of the open stairway barking. But she didn't move from that spot. She just stared upward whining.

"Who is it, Brigitte?" I asked the dog in an urgent tone, trying to get her to go upstairs. She was rarely afraid of anything, but she just stood there whining and wagging her tail nervously like she wanted me to go up first instead.

Some guard dog you are, I thought as I yelled out, "Hello! Cheryl, are you up there? I didn't hear you come home."

I looked out the window at the street to see if her car was there, but the whole street out front was empty. I checked the back driveway to see if she might have parked there, but her car was nowhere around. She wasn't home.

I didn't really want to go upstairs to investigate, but the noise stopped abruptly anyway and the dog suddenly calmed down. So I watched TV for a while that evening and got ready for bed.

But as I lay in bed reading my book that night, the dog that was lying on the floor lifted her head and flipped her ears toward the bedroom doorway. I stopped to listen and heard that same squeaking noise again in the hallway in that same spot in the floor.

"Hello," I yelled again. "Is anyone there?"

There was no answer. I convinced myself I was just hearing things or it was the house settling again, and I rolled over and went to sleep.

In the days that followed, I heard a lot of noises that I attributed to the house settling, but some strange things started to happen.

There was an old upright piano in the downstairs hallway that had been left with the house when I moved in. And I had arranged groups of family pictures on top of it. But strangely enough, one day I walked in to find one of the larger pictures lying face down on the floor in front of it. I wouldn't have thought it so strange but I had arranged the pictures in a staggered pattern and this one had been situated partially behind another picture that had oddly not been disturbed. I was puzzled, but I put the picture gently back into its place and I left for work as usual.

But later when I returned home, I was a bit shocked to find the same picture face down on the floor again in the same place, still with no other pictures in front of it having been moved. I was now starting to feel that something was very strange. No one else had been in the house, no one else except my traveling roommate had a key, and nothing else had been moved.

Several more weeks passed. I heard the strange footsteps periodically and occasionally found something around the house that had been moved. I tried to think of a way to dismiss it all as being normal, but one event made that impossible.

One night as I was sleeping, I suddenly awoke to the feeling of something at the end of the bed, like someone sitting on the corner near my feet. A little surge of adrenaline rushed over me as I struggled to focus in the dark room, but I saw nothing. I thought it must have been the dog moving around in the dark and I went back to sleep.

Then, a very short time later, maybe ten or fifteen minutes, I woke up again to the dog nudging me and whining anxiously. I tried to open my eyes and look at the clock but it was flashing. Had the electricity gone off? I scolded the dog for waking me up and sent her back to bed. And I rolled over and tried to go back to sleep.

A while later, my heart skipped a beat when I suddenly heard a pounding on the front door. I didn't want to answer the door alone in the middle of the night, but the dog had already run downstairs to the door and was barking in a more desperate tone than usual. I threw on my robe and ran downstairs. The pounding on the door continued furiously and I could see a dark silhouette of a figure outside with the street lights glowing behind it. I opened the door to see a fireman in full dress.

"Ma'am you need to get out of the house NOW. There's smoke coming from your attic window!"

I sat outside with the dog in the chill of twilight in late October as the firemen diffused a small electrical fire that had started from old, frayed wiring in the attic.

Luckily they had caught it in time and the damage was minimal, but I couldn't get the strange nagging feeling out of my head that someone had been sitting at the foot of the bed that night.

But the strangeness wasn't over yet.

After the repairs to the house were done and everything was quiet again, something else happened. There was an extra room on the main level in the house with bookshelves that I called the reading room, and I had all of my books arranged on its many shelves around the fireplace.

I was sitting in a chair in that room one afternoon reading my book when something suddenly made me look up. As I did, my big, thick dictionary suddenly flew from the shelf and dropped onto the hardwood floor several feet away from the shelf. If it had been a smaller, lighter book I might have thought it had simply fallen. But this was a huge, heavy, collegiate Merriam-Webster version. And it looked like something had just flicked it off the shelf violently and into the middle of the hardwood floor.

I guess this should have scared me, but I'd had a friend tell me her true ghost stories before many times, I didn't really believe them before, but now I was really wondering. It just seemed like something or someone was trying to be noticed. And I couldn't really think of another explanation for a book flying off a shelf.

After giving it some thought, I decided to go to the county courthouse and see if I could find some information about the previous owners of the house.

I took part of an afternoon off and went to the courthouse and local library and I sifted through old records and newspapers for any information about the previous occupants of the house. When I finally found some information, it was fairly boring - no dramatic murders, suicides, or mysterious deaths, but there had been local fire chief who had owned the house some fifty years before that had died at a fairly young age of pneumonia. Could he be the one haunting my house for some reason? Unfortunately, I couldn't find any more information on him, but he was the only individual that I found that had died an untimely death in the house.

Weeks went by again and the strange noises and events slowed down a little. Brigitte had a litter of puppies in the basement and I was up and down the basement stairs frequently checking on them. One day I was down there cleaning when I heard a loud slamming of the front door upstairs on the main level. I wasn't too disturbed because it was a small town and no one kept their doors locked during the day. I immediately thought it might be my dad or one of my friends coming in but no one had ever slammed the door so loudly.

I listened for a moment as heavy footsteps walked across the floor above my head from the front door all the way to the kitchen. It sounded like heavy boots on the hardwood, and I didn't move for a moment, trying to get a sense of who it might be. Brigitte, who was always a good watchdog, paid no attention as I listened to the footsteps shuffling around the kitchen. So I believed that if she wasn't disturbed by the visitor, it must be safe.

I suddenly felt curious enough to investigate and I headed up the stairs. As I faced the back door, I thought I saw a figure out of the corner of my eye through the door glass, but when I tried to focus, there was nothing there.

By that time I had convinced myself that this was the spirit of the young fire chief trying to make his presence known, and I was strangely unafraid as long he showed no animosity toward me.

I pushed the back door open and walked into the kitchen where the noises had come from. I thought I heard more strange shuffling as I came in, but it abruptly stopped as I closed the door behind me. The room became strangely quiet.

"Is there anyone here?" I asked. No one answered, but I kept talking.

"I know you're here and I know who you are, and I don't have a problem with your being here as long as I never actually see you."

It was the truth. But I believed that he hadn't really wanted to scare me to death. In the beginning he had subtly moved things around in the house, and perhaps when I failed to believe what was happening, he threw a dictionary off the shelf.

It had seemed that he just wanted to be noticed. I hoped what I said would appease him in some way, and I also hoped that, if he was real, he understood that it was important that I never ever actually, physically laid eyes on him.

Was it a ghost of the fire chief who had died in the house all those years ago? Was there some correlation between his being a fireman and the house catching on fire that night? Had he been trying to warn me in some gentle way?

After that day, things seemed to become quiet in the old house. There were no other noises or activities except for a few strange, small thumps every now and then. It's almost like he relaxed a bit at me being there.

INDIANA

AS TOLD BY: CHRISTIAN HUTCHENS

It was said that Cora Waltman was an unstable woman. She was married and had children. She died at a very young age due to suicide. Supposedly she hung herself in the doorway of what used to be my bedroom on the second floor. The reason why she hung herself was to protect her family from herself. It is rumored that she heard voices in her head that told her to kill her husband and children.

The house was built in the 1880s. Before we moved in, many people had told me the house was haunted. They said that they had heard things in the house. Others said they saw a woman in the window upstairs. One person I knew even said when she was in the window, she bore an ax. I didn't think much of it.

Once we moved in, I didn't stay upstairs until about six months after the move-in. When I was upstairs, I started hearing what sounded like footsteps going up and down the stairs. Sometimes they were slow, and other times it sounded like running. I didn't take this too seriously because it was an old house and the wooden steps creaked when you went up or down them. I assumed it was just normal house noises. It happened often and I only heard them at night.

There are also many accounts of things coming up missing. The strangest was when my mother set a bracelet down in her room on a table. Three of us watched her place it there. When we got home from a funeral it was missing. A week later the bracelet reappeared exactly where it was.

This is where it gets more interesting. When I was living there I used to own a D.J. business. I had a bunch of strobe lights. One night I was walking by and one of them was flashing (I had left two plugged in, but turned off). It was flashing as fast as it could. I checked it and it was off so I unplugged it and went back to bed. A couple of hours later, I was awakened again. This time it was the other strobe light across the room doing the same thing the other one was doing. I checked it and it was turned to the slowest speed. This happened a number of times. I used different strobes and they would come on in the middle of the night. One night I was sleeping through it and my mother woke me up and two of them (different strobes than the original ones) were flashing as fast as they could.

Another night me and a friend were sitting in my room watching television. The remote sat on a small table just out of our reach. All of a sudden the sound started going up. We sat and watched the volume go up from 20-38 or so. We sat and looked at each other scratching our heads. A couple minutes passed by and we turned our attention to the television again. Then the volume went back down by itself from 38 back to 20, right where it left off. We were pretty confused by that time.

One night I was sleeping and I had turned the television off before I went to sleep. I woke up in the middle of the night to the sound of the television on. It had a snowy picture, even though the satellite was on and working. When I looked closer, the image of a woman's face seemed to appear. At first it was hard to see, but soon you could see the shape very well. I stared for a moment and noticed it looked like it was moving. It took a few minutes of being in awe before I finally unplugged it and went back to sleep. This happened again - the same thing, but this time the face was very visible. This time I went and got my mother and let her see it. It freaked her out as well. And she drives a hearse for her personal transportation, so it takes a lot to get her freaked.

The most interesting time was when I still lived there and my current girlfriend came over to visit. We were sitting around late at night. We had heard the steps a few times and ignored it as always. I had never really told her that the house might be haunted at all. She was pregnant at the time. We had fallen asleep and she woke up and said she saw a woman. She wasn't sure so she rubbed her eyes and she was gone. She said it looked like she was hanging at the doorway. The doorway to the bedroom is where Cora Waltman supposedly had hung herself. My girlfriend was not sure if she was hanging or standing, but said it appeared she was hanging or hovering.

There have been people who say they've felt cold, got a cold chill, and so on. There also was another death. I can't remember his name but he died at the very top of stairs from a heart attack.

I believe there is an entity that is a ghost there, and I believe it to be Cora Waltman.

IOWA

AS TOLD BY: GENE WHEELDON

I had moved to Bartlett, Iowa back in 1938 when I was just 11 years old. Little did I know all of the experiences that would lie ahead of me. Back before the depression, Bartlett was a booming town with a lot to offer, but sadly many businesses were shut down that couldn't stand to stay in business due to hard economic times. We were left with one gas station and one grocery store.

One night when I was between the ages of twelve and fourteen, my buddies Merv Foster and Butch Morrison were all hanging out in town. There was an old abandoned building that used to be a funeral parlor that was rumored to be "haunted". Many people in town had always said they had seen reflections and candle lights in the window with shadowy figures, but no one dared to go in. Being the young whippersnapper daredevils we were, we all decided about 11 p.m. we would go in and see for ourselves if this place was really haunted.

After breaking in through the side door, we walked to an entryway to see upstairs - the part that was supposedly "haunted". We all carefully walked to the entryway and were about to head up the stairs, but we all froze. As I looked up to start climbing the stairs, there it was. As best as I can describe it, there was a white smoky silver light in an upright position in the form of a person. There was no face, but it definitely resembled a person.

We all stood there shaking in our britches. We stared at this figure for what seemed about 15 seconds before we bolted out the way we came. We were absolutely terrified and never went back. Although it was scary at the time, throughout the years Butch, Merv, and I would reminisce about that night, and it sure does make for a great story.

KANSAS

AS TOLD BY: ANONYMOUS

I was 8 years old and a friend brought over an Ouija board for our sleep-over.

We drew a black pentagram on it thinking it would connect us to something, not knowing it was a portal to the other side. Nothing happened at first but then the board actually worked.

I was so convinced my friend was doing it until she let go and it kept moving around. Immediately I got scared and asked a few questions, but it would give us random names for things that made no sense. When I Googled them later it was the name of a church in a small religious town in the south. With research, I found the church used to be the meeting place of a cult and all their crimes.

My friend went home and the next weekend we tried again. I remember we had the Ouija board in my room and I was teasing her because she was too scared to try again so I said, "I invite any and all beings to come here but you cannot harm my family or pets. Show me you're here."

Nothing happened but, this time a bad thing actually did happen. She did the Ouija board with me again.

When we did it we could hear heavy breathing and feel it burning our cheeks and my friend Rhianna got what looked like a cold chill and got really quiet. I asked if she was okay and she looked up at me with huge pupils and a voice came out that wasn't hers, that said, "I want to hurt you," and then she started choking and crying and ran and turned on the lights.

She said she didn't feel like she could control herself and she needs to go home because she doesn't want to harm me but she does. I left the board under my bed and we forgot to say goodbye.

For years two entities harassed me. One was very bad and I had to be exorcised because it would wake me up holding me down and break my dogs leg, or once it ripped all the posters off my wall and flew them like a tornado around me cutting me all over.

I got it banished from my home after many attempts over many years.

The other was protective over me. It was a male I know because it shook me awake and yelled at me trying to tell me something but it talked too fast to understand. When it wanted to communicate, it would wake me but I couldn't move and it always scared me but it never physically harmed me.

It would follow me day and night in the house.

I would be home alone and hear my bird in the kitchen talking to the presence. I would come to the cage and the cabinet would be open, treats open, and the bird would be eating a treat that someone would have had to give her.

Sometimes it would knock on my door and open it. Over time I learned to live in harmony with it and would respect it instead of threaten it. But if I brought a friend or boy over, they would be attacked. It wanted me to itself. It burned a weird mark into my sister's side that didn't heal for two months. I looked it up and it was a demonic symbol for demon.

It did that to her when she tried to smudge my room because she would get sick whenever she walked into it. The demon would follow me to school, work, etc, like it was my guard dog.

I can never get rid of it. I just moved to Oklahoma and it's gotten a lot less clingy because there is a protection spell on this house, but I know it's still there.

KENTUCKY

AS TOLD BY: DANNY HOWELL

I was working in a wilderness area years ago when, while driving into the jobsite, my car struck a huge rock knocking a hole in my oil pan. I was miles from the nearest house. I didn't have a cell phone, and only my wife and my boss knew where I was at. But they would not be looking for me for hours.

I decided to walk to the closest house to see if they would let me use the phone to call home. It was becoming dark now. As I walked out of the middle of nowhere, I remembered driving by an old cemetery on my way in. When I got within 50 feet of the cemetery, I could hear people talking in a low tone. I thought, "good, someone can give me a ride." I walked up to the cemetery still hearing voices. No one was there, but I could still hear talking. I took off running. The voices got louder until I got to the edge of the driveway of the house just down the road, then the voices stopped. I turned around but there was nobody there. I ran to the front door of the house, trying to calm down so they would not think I was a nut. I used their phone, and my wife came and got me. I never told her or anyone.

I went back the next day to fix my car, I didn't hear or see anything. I fixed my car and got out of there. I told my boss I could not work in this area anymore, but he said that was the only job he had going. I told him I guess I quit then. I never went back.

LOUISIANA

AS TOLD BY: Parrish Gore

Since childhood I have lived on this dead end street in the middle of Walker, Louisiana. Few homes line the pavement on this quarter mile stretch of roadway.

The vast space of emptiness between the houses grows rather dark at night and with the wooded areas surrounding the neighborhood, Fletcher Lane has the appearance of an old country road deep in the woods.

There are no street lights to brighten the nights, no illumination from local businesses, there is only the darkness and subtle sounds of silence.

Over the years many families have moved here. Some families moved into the neighborhood and moved away. A few that stayed lived here until their deaths. There are those who died in the very home they lived in.

Being such a secluded neighborhood, everyone that lived on Fletcher Lane became like family. A close knit community I suppose one could surmise. Given that, when someone passes on to the next world it has an emotional effect on everyone.

I've always been a somewhat spiritual person, matters of the afterlife and the existence of spirits amongst the living have intrigued me. Though I've had some experiences, for the most part my personal opinion and theory regarding the supernatural has been limited to the experiences of others.

I have developed some opinions from these collective experiences. One is that the fabric between this world and the next is not woven very thick. Another is the belief that emotions play a significant role in the connection between the living and the dead - to what extent I can only ponder.

As a living creature I understand things of this world, this life. I understand emotions like pain, sadness, happiness, and joy - emotions both good and bad. But what of those who've passed on to the afterlife? Are they here? If so, do they still feel the emotions they did when alive? Do they recognize the living? Do they linger with a sense of fulfillment or solemn loneliness? Do they remember?

The answer to these questions I can only theorize. Yet I have experienced events that cannot be explained using logic or rational thought. The story I am about to tell is a true story, and one that has helped me better understand how to answer these questions.

It was the summer of 1973 when my family moved to Fletcher Lane. There was a family living across the street from us, an older couple, with a son who had just recently arrived home from the Vietnam War.

I was 9 years old then, and immediately discovered an affection for this family. I was especially fond of their son, Tommy.

Though he was much older than I, Tommy seemed like the older brother I never had. His tales of the jungles of Vietnam and the experiences of war enthralled the wide-eyed child that I was. For the entire summer of 1973 I became a shadow to Tommy, learning different things. Once he taught me how to make a table from a tree trunk.

It was adventurous in a way, and somewhat therapeutic for me since I had left all my friends from the old neighborhood. And since there were no children my age in the neighborhood, following Tommy around was really all there was for me to do.

Then one day, as I was helping Tommy cut firewood for the winter, a question arose in my thoughts. A question any child, or any adult for that matter, would wonder. My question was, "What's it like to kill somebody?"

He was splitting logs with an axe when I asked him.

At first I thought he was angry with me because he came to a halt in mid swing and said nothing. I stared for a moment, sweat dripped from the red bandanna wrapped around Tommy's forehead. After a few moments he gently lowered the axe and looked into the woods with a blank expression on his face. Shame suddenly rushed through my body and I lowered my head. The dry leaves and twigs covering the ground offered no solace to the way I was feeling. The feeling I had suddenly invaded his privacy washed through my thoughts.

But after a few minutes, Tommy looked at me and shared something I'll never forget. He told me a tale of something that happened while he was in Vietnam.

At the time I didn't quite understand the complexity of the events, but as I got older I did.

Tommy explained that he was part of an engineer platoon. Their responsibility was to clear land for troops. The danger of this responsibility was grave. Constantly under scrutiny from the enemy and, without a leader who has experience, their life expectancy was lowered.

During Tommy's first few months, their Lieutenant was savvy and knowledgeable regarding the operations of the Platoon. He listened to his men and made sound tactical decisions that kept the level of danger to a minimum. It was after this Lieutenant completed his tour that things got bad.

As Tommy explained, the new Lieutenant was fresh out of Officer Training School and his attitude was arrogant. He wouldn't listen to the soldiers who had been in the jungle for a good period of time. This caused the Platoon to be put in dangerous situations and in some circumstances, men were killed. The stress level of the men grew with each passing day. Nerves were frayed, and they felt drastic measures needed to be taken to rectify the situation. Tommy explained that this Lieutenant was unapproachable. When several of the enlisted men attempted to confer with the Lieutenant about his mentality and attitude they were threatened with court martial.

With this form of treatment, the men within the Platoon lost trust and faith in their leader. How can a man be expected to follow someone who shows no respect or concern for his subordinates?

It was what Tommy explained next that sent chills through my body. Straws were drawn, one man chosen, a deed that must be done. And it was Tommy who was chosen to carry out the deed.

It was late and the jungle grew darker as the sun gradually set in the distant western sky. The sky was the color of blood as Tommy explained.

In my mind I envisioned a dark red sky, the clouds dripping in the western horizon. Slowly dripping like blood from a small wound.

There was a quiet solemn mood about the campsite. All the men retreated to their tents, and there they waited.

Tommy had set himself away from the other men. Sitting alone beneath a Bonsai tree, Tommy waited. He told me his thoughts were nearly absent as he glared into the blood sky. He told me that he heard nothing. No artillery fire in the distance, no sounds that the jungle makes at night, he heard nothing. Nothing but the beating of his own heart as it pounded against the bones in his chest. He had reached such a level of focus and concentration, not even the mosquitoes feasting on the back of his neck were noticeable. And in his hands, as the last glimmer of daylight sank into the jungle, the machete he would use.

The nights were as hot as the days in the jungles of Vietnam. Sometimes it would rain, but the rain was warm and offered no relief to the heat.

Sweat drenched Tommy's clothes as he rose from beneath the Bonsai tree. Each step was calculated and methodical as he eased closer and closer to the Lieutenant's tent. If anyone took notice of Tommy, they remained silent. Once he reached the Lieutenant's quarters, Tommy listened. There the faint sound of sleep in the quiet confines. Tommy walked cautiously towards the cot where the lieutenant lay. Once there, and positioned, with just enough light from a lantern hung from the ceiling behind the Lieutenants bed, Tommy did the deed that needed to be done.

There was one point during the brief scuffle that ensued where Tommy told me the Lieutenant opened his eyes. The glare was horrifying as Tommy explained. A glare as unnatural as any he had witnessed before or after.

From that moment on, Tommy told me he has nightmares about killing the Lieutenant. He said there are times he feels as if the spirit of the Lieutenant follows him around, haunting his nights.

What Tommy said about killing someone, the answer to my question, is it feels like a part of you dies as well. Like an area of your being that makes you feel human is suddenly gone. And it creates a place in your heart where there is emptiness. He told me it was difficult to explain and it was even more difficult for a 9 year old to understand. As I've matured, so has my understanding, but the full extent of understanding I hope to never know.

Later that evening, after the firewood was cut and I helped Tommy with a few more chores, he showed me the machete he had used. Tommy told me he never used the machete again. He said he placed it on the bottom of his footlocker and brought it home. Where in his trailer he kept it I was never told. Often I've wondered why he kept it. I never asked that question, though he had his reasons I'm sure.

And that same machete is at the core of my experience.

Tommy lived next door to his parents the rest of their lives. They both died within a year of each other in the early 2000s.

It was in March of 2006 when Tommy died. He had several problems with his health and it eventually caused his death. I visited as often as I could, but being married with four children of my own left little time to socialize. Tommy died in his trailer one Sunday morning.

The coroner wasn't sure as to the cause and no autopsy was performed because foul play wasn't suspected. But it was believed he died after suffering a stroke.

I still wonder if he had a nightmare that was so severe it caused his stroke. The spirit of the Lieutenant haunting his dreams. I guess that sounds like foolishness, but who knows?

A few years after Tommy's death, my nephew bought his trailer and land. Of course he was aware that Tommy died in the trailer, and I suppose that is one reason Tommy's family had trouble selling the place. But it was such a good price my nephew couldn't pass it up.

It was one late afternoon when I walked next door to visit with my nephew that something happened and it still brings chills to my body when I think about it.

Friday afternoon, late October just before 6 p.m., I walked to Tommy's trailer to visit my nephew. It was dark, like it always gets on Fletcher Lane at night. But even in the dark I noticed something odd.

Above the trailer and towards the middle, there seemed to be a large cloud of smoke. My nephew didn't have a chimney or stove pipe extending above the roof so I was somewhat curious. At first, I thought maybe he had started a fire in the back yard. I made my way to the rear of the trailer but there was no fire. I didn't smell the pungent scent of a fire, either. Then I realized my nephew wasn't home from work yet. Suddenly I thought the trailer itself was on fire. I quickly surveyed the outside and saw nothing that indicated the trailer was burning.

I called my nephew on my cell phone but for some reason there was no signal. I found this perplexing because there was a satellite antenna just half a mile away and I knew he should be on the way home. After a few more attempts to contact my nephew, I decided there was no imminent danger. Had the trailer been on fire I would have seen a blaze or something by then. It was totally dark by now; the moon was full and bright.

There was some illumination coming through the kitchen window, so I sat on the back door steps, stared at the sky, and waited. Given the time of night, I knew my nephew would be home soon. Just a couple hours before I had talked to him.

So I put everything from my thoughts and sat quietly waiting. I'm not sure why I decided to wait there in the dark. Usually I would have walked back to my house across the street and came back later.

But I didn't.

Several minutes passed before something happened. It sent a shiver through my body, and I felt a presence. It wasn't exactly like how you feel when you think you're being watched. It was more like the sensation when you're alone at night, in your bedroom. The door is closed and you're trying to sleep, but you suddenly feel as though someone is in the room with you. It's the kind of feeling that causes you to lay there, motionless, afraid to move or speak. And the longer you think about the sensation the more intense it becomes.

I couldn't move my head to look around the back yard. I could make out the shapes of bushes and the two trees in the yard, but I could see nothing in the darkness around them. The darkness took on the personification of shadows. Like they were living beings, dressed in the blackness of the night, hiding. I just felt petrified. My body motionless and quiet.

Then, without warning, I heard it. But it was no sound in the yard, no sound behind the trees or bushes, it came from inside the trailer. It was in the bedroom. Just beyond the reach of the back door, and it startled me. I listened intently, not as much from curiosity, but rather forcefully.

From the volume and direction of the sound it seemed to be coming from the bedroom closet. A faint sound of scuffling, moving small things around. The sounds weren't constant, there were breaks between them. And the sounds weren't loud. If I were to start talking on the phone I don't think I could have heard them.

This lasted a few minutes. Then there was silence again. My back was to the back door. Behind the back door, in the trailer, was the small laundry area. To the right of the laundry area was the master bedroom. The same room I heard the noises in; the same room Tommy died in.

Moments of silence quickly surrendered to a different nature of sound. The doorway from the bedroom to the laundry area was just a couple feet from the back door. What I heard next was even more startling. It sounded like footsteps, and after each step there was a dragging noise. As if someone were walking across the bedroom and towards the bedroom doorway. The dragging of feet with each step. Again the sounds were faint. Almost undetectable. Then, the sounds changed, like walking on carpet then onto a hard floor. And when the sound reached the back door, just behind where

I sat, it stopped. Again there was silence. My heart was pounding and my hands shook. I didn't think I could catch my breath.

Deep within my thoughts I wanted to turn and look, but I couldn't. The thought of something glaring at me through the small window in the door circled in my mind. An intense and indescribable sensation gripped me. Like the feeling of being watched but more realistic than before. Almost as if it were stalking me. Waiting for the right moment, then, when all is calm, attacking. An attack with such a voracious need the aftermath would be epic.

How long this feeling and the silence lasted, I do not know. All sense of time was drawn from me. Eventually the silence ended. Then, I heard them again, but now they were going in the direction of the kitchen. The quiet, slow, almost ominous sound of footfalls and feet being slid across the floor. There was a part of me that wanted this to be my imagination. The wind playing tricks on my mind. Yet there were no winds. The night was calm and still.

Brief were the sounds going into the kitchen, brief and then nothing again. Listening without the desire to hear, I waited. There were no more footfalls, no dragging or sliding of feet across floor, nothing. My eyes remained fixated on the shadows in the backyard. Those areas of darkness where anything could be hiding and would go undetected. I simply stared as my thoughts pondered the idea that something could be lurking within the pitch of night. Something could be waiting in the trailer.

It was at that moment, just as my nephew's truck turned into the driveway, I saw it. From somewhere to my right, behind a tree beside the trailer, maybe, in some way, through the window from inside the trailer, it moved.

Describing its movement is difficult. I cannot say it flew - there were no wings - but it moved fast, in the blink of an eye. It moved towards me and then straight up into the dark sky.

It was the size of a basketball, white but not solid white. I'd never in my life seen anything that resembled this thing. I call it a thing because I am beyond any doubt positive it was no object. Though I feel it was no tangible object, I am at a loss to determine what the nature of its composition could be.

The following day I contacted a friend who currently lives in Colorado. He conducts paranormal investigations and has had many experiences with situations of this nature. I explained to Sam what I had experienced and what I saw. He directed me to his website and there I saw photos of things that resembled the thing that moved through the air. I also saw things that resembled the white cloud above the trailer when I walked from across the street.

When I explained what photos resembled the thing I saw he told me that is an Orb. When I saw it on the roof, it appeared as a Super Charged Orb. A Super Charged Orb is the manifestation of a spirit in a mist like form with a pink, blue or green hue.

What I saw as I sat on the back steps was an Ecto Orb. As I recalled the thing moving through the air, it almost seems as though it had a face. It's difficult to be sure because it happened so quickly. But an Ecto Orb will at times attempt to manifest itself to resemble what it looked like while in human form.

These terms and descriptions were offered to me from my friend. I'm not certain as to who this orb was. But there was one last thing that my nephew and I discovered that night, and it was this that frightened me more than anything else.

After my nephew pulled his truck to the rear of his trailer, I explained what had taken place. He of course thought I was crazy, laughing as he invited me inside. After going through the back doorway he went into the kitchen, I wandered into his bedroom. I couldn't tell if anything was out of place or not.

But after a few seconds my nephew called for me. His voice was somewhat nervous and alarmed.

I made my way into the kitchen, where he was standing beside the breakfast counter, his back to me. He seemed to be staring at the countertop. When

I walked around to his side so I could see the countertop, I saw what he was staring at.

It was the machete.

The same one Tommy had shown me years before. My nephew was bewildered as was I. He asked me if I had placed the machete on there, to which I replied no, of course.

But the chill running through my veins was so profound I could barely stand. It was at that moment I realized what and who I saw - it was Tommy, or rather his ghost or spirit or whatever term one may apply.

Because of our close relationship I suppose he was attempting to make contact. Trying to let me know he was still here. That's why I sometimes wonder to what extent emotions play in the manifestation of spirits.

That was several months ago, I have not seen any signs of Tommy since then. Even though my nephew threw the machete away, he discarded any idea of a supernatural or paranormal event. Rather deciding one of his girlfriend's children had found the machete and placed it on the countertop. Both children denied the accusation.

But I cannot find this rationale within my conscious thoughts. What I sensed and felt was real. What I saw was real. And since then there are nights, as I lay in bed in the darkness of my room, I hear things. At times objects will fall from my dresser, or my bookshelf. Objects that have no known force causing them to fall. I wonder if it's Tommy. I wonder if he's lonely and attempting to let me know he's here. One thing I do know, and this I feel beyond a shadow of a doubt, the living are not alone. The spirits are among us.

MAINE

AS TOLD BY: KEVIN P. TREMBLAY

I purchased the Lane Homestead at the 45th parallel in Ripley, Somerset County, Maine, and moved here from Boston nearly thirty years ago. The farmer selling me the place, Rudy Goulette, had a few stories to pass along with the deed. One was about the gold coins buried on the place from the hoarding bachelor Cooley, who had lived on the farm all his adult life as a hired hand, and about a ghostly presence. Cooley tended the milk cows, put up firewood and helped with haying. Cooley also owned a wood lot across the way from here Rudy said, and worked the lot when he had time off from farm chores. He had horses to pull the timber and boarded them on the farm too.

Cooley had no expenses except the bare necessities. He received room and board and saved the stipend from working on the farm, and the money he made off of his wood lot. That is how he came to have the gold coins he buried here. This was before Rudy's time, and his daughter Gail had this to say, "Cooley was a strange guy, he hoarded his money." He did not believe in banks. No one now living knew him, but the stories of his hiding his gold on the farm linger on.

Rudy purchased the farm from an heir of Stora Kimball, Edward A. Pearl, on October 15, 1954. Rudy originally owned the Page place next door, but it didn't have enough land for him to get a loan from the Farmer Home Administration to run a dairy farm, and what he wanted to do, so he looked into buying this place. The Lane Homestead had been abandoned and closed up for about a decade.

The Town of Ripley placed a lien on the property for unpaid taxes in 1945 and again in 1946. Stora must have died, as the lien mentions that a letter was sent to him at his last known address in Ripley and uses the language, "that a demand for payment of said tax... [by or through the] executor-administrator-heir-devisee," indicating knowledge of his death.

The property consisted of open pasture land of about fifty acres for a total of two hundred acres that went with the place. Rudy, and his wife Phyllis, made a deal with the heir in Massachusetts to purchase the property through owner financing. However, before Pearl would sell it to him, some of the heirs came here in 1954 with a metal detector and scoured the place looking for the gold. Rudy said they even pulled the walls apart looking for the cache of gold coins. But they had no luck he surmised, as they never said, and Pearl transferred the place to him.

Within a few years Rudy and Phyllis paid the mortgage off to Ralph W. Pearl, Administrator of

Edward Pearl's estate as Edward had died in the interim. The property had been paid off, but there was still a debt to pay!

Rudy mentioned to me that the home was haunted. "Nothing bad ever happened, but sometimes it felt as if there was a man looking over my shoulder." Then added, "That's what folks said anyhow, that the place was haunted. I never saw anything, but you'll find out what I mean. I got spooked a few times." I did find out what he meant.

This place has history. The house is circa 1847, but I am not positive about the date as it was difficult to follow the transfers of the property at the Registry of Deeds. A few deeds referred to the property as the Moses L. Arno home place, who may have been one of the original owners from the 1830s. In any event the original settlers cleared the land for crops and grazing cattle, and keeping horses. Rudy said that one of the Lane daughters married Stora Kimball early 1900s, and Stora ran the place until he got sick and died with no one to take over the farm. That was until Rudy bought the place.

There had been a slaughterhouse here a long time ago, in the barn across the street that has since fallen in. That is how Rudy believed a safe got to be here, and how he got into trouble with the law. When Rudy moved from the contiguous Page place to here some stuff was left behind by the heirs. One was a safe that was broken open. He thought that with all the money the Lane's handled from running the slaughterhouse, they needed a safe; and there were the hired hands and summer crew to consider.

The slaughterhouse was a gathering spot for the cattle in the area at roundup time, that were going for the fall trek to the Boston market. This was a distance of over two hundred miles. The cattle were herded all the way to the city from Ripley. Rudy also told me about the truck loads of whiskey, beer bottles and cans he carted off to the dump that were emptied out of the barn. The barn was still chuck-full of booze bottles when I got here thirty-two years after him. They were stuffed in the space between the whitewashed barn ceiling and floor above for the hay.

These bottles, cans and the safe that Rudy took to the Dexter town dump got him into trouble. As his daughter Gail said, "There was the story about the safe that dad found here that was broken. He dumped it at the Dexter dump. The Dexter Chief of Police at the time was Harold Knox. He came out to ask dad about the safe. They thought that someone had broken into a bank or something, and dumped the safe. They traced it back to Rudy and came out to talk to him about this." Rudy told me about this himself and said that the cops tried to imply that it was crime to dump a safe like that. He told Officer Knox to go away.

Then Gail and her brother Peter talked about the dynamite found hidden upstairs. Apparently the dynamite was used in clearing the fields, to break up the ledge and granite found in the land. Peter said, "Look along the stonewall and you will find where they had drilled into the stone to place the dynamite to break up the bigger rock." This might account for the granite in the newer part of the foundation of this cape style farmhouse, a rambling New Englander.

The neighbor Frank Spizuoco, a local historian, told me about the demise of John Lane, the former owner, who purchased the property from Benjamin Chandler in 1883. "John died in a logging accident in 1911 between here and the Page place next door." There were a number of people that died while living here over the last one hundred and sixty years and Cooley, the gold hoarder, had been one of them. He died in one of the bedrooms upstairs.

Over the years there have been many experiences that have unnerved me and two of my tenants told me about what happened to them. I rent rooms and have had a number of people live here, some for years. Both these tenants stayed in the "bad door" room which I will explain. When I first came here there were a number of incidents that indicated some kind of a presence. The most significant was the unlatching door. The bedrooms upstairs have antique rod iron style door latches. A flattened iron rod falls into a slot when the latch is released, or when the door is shut the rod slides into the slot which is attached to the door frame. You have to click it up and out of the slot to open the door. One room in particular the door would never stay shut for very long. The door was not found wide open, just unlatched and open a few inches. During the most active point the door would not stay latched for more than a day. For periods of time I have lived here alone, and so there was no one to blame for the door being opened when I had shut and latched it a day or two before.

This section of the house is very sturdy and level so it could not be accounted for by a give in the floor that would unlatch it and the wind could not unlatch it. For a while I would take particular note making sure the doors to the bedrooms upstairs were all shut. There are four bedrooms facing into the hall and staircase with a window above the stairs.

One day I had been downstairs in the front room lying on the couch watching TV and heard the latch click open. The hairs stood up on the back of my neck and gooseflesh appeared on my arms and legs. A cold chill traveled through me. I was freaked out. These things rarely seem to happen in the evening. It was in the afternoons that there were the strongest feelings of supernatural activity.

I had to face this fear of whoever or whatever was upstairs. In the past I had closed the door and expressed out loud that I did not want the door to be opened again. This time I flew up the stairs to the door and waving my finger at the door after closing it and yelled, "You bad door, stay shut." I said a few prayers. No one was there of course. There are things that are out of our understanding, and this is one of them for me. There is no explaining how the door becomes unlatched on its own.

The particular tenants previously mentioned stayed in this room with the bad door. Tammy rented here for about six months. One morning she asked me if I had come into her bedroom over night. I had not. Then she went on to explain that someone had sat on her bed while she slept which really upset her.

Phil, the other tenant, said the same thing happened to him. He rented here for a number of years. He felt someone sit on his bed while he was in it a few times. Phil also said that many times when he came home from work, the door to his room had been opened, when he had left it latched before going off in the mornings. He thought that I had been going in his room. When we talked about the door being opened and someone sitting on his bed he became unnerved.

Another tenant renting here that had paranormal experiences was Neil. He thought he saw a ghost. He rented the room beside the "bad door" one. Neil saw an aberration walk through his room. "I thought I saw something walk through my room." One time he was home alone and had shut the bedroom door next to his, and shortly later the door was open. Neil said, "There was no breeze, the window was closed, and I know I closed the door, and somebody opened it. I felt there is a spirit in the house. Not an evil one, just a spirit."

Diane, a friend from Chicago that stays at the farm a few times a year, was sleeping in the blue room across from the bad door room. As she explained, "I had been asleep and felt someone pull a cover over me, but they didn't. I had been cold and pulled the covers over myself. Something floated through the room and out the window. It was so real. I did not see her, but felt a presence. It was very peaceful and definitely a woman."

It has been my etheric observation that the entity opens the door and crosses the hallway to this blue room to look out into the dooryard or goes through the other bedroom to the far end of the house.

Peter, Rudy's son had a scary experience. "Once everyone was gone, I had been haying with Spook, and came home. I was watching TV in the living room and the doors upstairs kept slamming. I heard someone talking upstairs. It was weird. I was 15 or 16 at the time. I'm 52. It was a long time ago. The door kept slamming. Rudy use to sleep in that room at the top of the stairs. It's true, it was back in 1975." Gail said that the door that kept slamming was the same door as the "bad door." Peter ran up the street to his older brother John's trailer that was about 2,000 feet up Chandler Hill Road barefoot.

Being so frightened by this experience he left his shoes behind.

Peter also said that, "One of the Cooleys died up in one of the bedrooms. His room was at the top of the stairs on the left. He died in that room... Kimball was the boozer. He used to drink Oxhead Ale. Kimball was sick and had someone that used to take care of him. Rudy bought the place from the heirs of Stora Kimball. He was really sick. He may have died here too." If there are ghosts is it Stora or Cooley or someone else that passed through the veil here?

One day while out in the garden weeding, I headed for the house to get a drink and to take a break from the hot sun. As I entered the dooryard from out behind the barn I looked up into the window in the blue room. This bedroom faces into the dooryard and to the southwest. There was a man standing there in the window with a woman behind him looking out. No, not real people, not flesh and blood humans, but the image of them in the ether as watery figures in my subconscious. I saw them all the same. Upon coming into the house, I went right upstairs to the room. No one was there. There have been other times sitting upstairs reading when it felt as if someone had passed by me. There would be a wisp, a whoosh, and then a curtain would move unexpectedly. Yes, a breeze could explain the curtain's movement. No, I did not see a person, or "see" a ghost, just the hint of one, or something ethereal. Not of this world.

At times there has been the form of a woman glimpsed at the edge of my conscious mind, as a dream figure. When outside looking in the windows of this old farmhouse is when the forms became most manifest. When inside the house these experiences are typically more sensual, not often visual or auditory. They are more sublime and out of my conscious mind. You might call these kinds of experiences "ethereal waking dreamscapes."

Other occurrences not ethereal add to the mystery. An interesting metal trivet was found in the woodshed under all the wood dust, bark and litter. Rocks were piled together for a door stoop going from the shed into the house. This trivet was discovered when shoveling out more than two feet of wood litter collected over the decades. Under the rocks and debris I discovered a rotting burlap bag. Wrapped within was this trivet. The rocks seemed placed on top to hold the trivet down. It looked sinister, first by being of a fiery design with two eyes and a ring on top; a demon consciousness. Why was it hidden like this? The ring on top was broken.

A friend believed that this trivet was circa 1820 and said it could have been used as an object lesson to teach children about Hell during mealtime. When a steaming pot from the wood stove was placed on it sitting on the kitchen table, the mother would talk about the fires down below. She might say that bad children, thieves and liars would go to that fiery place, "They would go to Hell."

Another case of the unexplained occurred in April 1996. A letter addressed to Stora Kimball was found on the ground outside the back door a few feet from the house. It was mid evening and I was going to the barn for something. There it was on the ground. At first I'd thought it was from my mailbox having been caught by a wind. Surprisingly, the letter was from Eastern Bank and Trust Co., Dexter, Maine and addressed to Stora L. Kimball, with a postmark dated April 24, 1914.

Dear Sir: -

We return herewith check from Knights of Maccabees of the World payable to your order, $15.00 which you have neglected to receipt. Please receipt same and return to us and we will credit your account.
Yours Respectfully,
Manager.

There had been a "Tent" for this fraternity, the Knights of the Maccabees of the World in Ripley, in the early 1900s. The Knights' meeting place was located on the second floor of the Ripley Creamery on Water Street. The building is gone. The Maccabees were a mutual benefit society which evolved into Maccabee Mutual Life Insurance Co., and eventually merged with Sun Royal. For this letter to appear in my dooryard eighty-two years later is inexplicable.

The letter is difficult to explain. Where had it come from? The only logical conclusion was the birds nesting within the eves of the house disturbed it from within the inner walls and the letter somehow got out and fell to the ground where I'd found it.

An interesting quality was noted about the letter. Most everyone that held it said it felt hot. Even I have to say that the longer I held it in the palm of my hand the hotter it became. Of eleven people that held the letter, all of them except Steve the skeptic, said it felt hot. He just looked surprised and tossed the letter back to me, saying, "What's up with this?" Steve would not commit even when told, after the test on him, what others had experienced. Over the years since it was found, the amount of heat emanating from the letter has progressively decreased.

This past year two Maine paranormal research teams investigated this property for paranormal activity. P.R.I.ME. (Paranormal Research In Maine) located in Bangor did their initial investigation on November 25, 2012. They returned for further testing and monitoring on May 11, 2013. The second group that investigated the property on January 12, 2013, was the East Coast Ghost Trackers, LLC also based in Bangor.

Both teams used digital audio recorders, IR night vision camera, EMF and temperature meters, two-way communication devices and other surveillance equipment, and East Coast Ghost Trackers used a Tesla coil. How cool is that? Both teams set up central operations in my kitchen, and monitors were placed in the room with the unlatching door and other rooms and in the basement.

In the first investigation P.R.I.ME reported that, "We found brief moments of EMF spikes while in the basement, readings being reported on both the K-II and Tri-field Meter." "The team upstairs documented their own K-II hits and heard tapping coming from the corner of the bedroom that they were investigating. Again, ultimately inconclusive," Nomar Slevik reported.

During the second investigation the team reported that they "began getting responsive EMF spikes," from the barn. Also there were "a few potential whispers and breaths" recorded. P.R.I.ME's conclusion was: "Based on another relatively quiet investigation, some interesting EVPs, and responsive EMF spikes in the barn we believe that more documentation is needed to deem this location haunted but, instances of the paranormal may be occurring." These two reports, video and sound from these investigations are on the Internet at the P.R.I.ME web page.

The East Coast Ghost Trackers were more directed in their investigation looking for ghosts. The investigation was being filmed as well as P.R.I.ME's investigations. They had these interesting digital voice box synthesizers that the entities could use to talk through apparently. One investigator engaged me in a discussion about my experiences while we stood in the old woodshed where the trivet was found. She held one of these devices and asked questions of any entities that may be present. At one point the voice synthesizer said the word "liar".

Then she noticed a book on the bookshelf about six feet away that appeared to be pulled out from the others. Strangely it was a Scholastic book by P. J. Peterson, Liars. The book beside this was Seth Speaks by Jane Roberts and was pulled out as well. At this point I became uncomfortable. My inclination is to have nothing to do with the channeled spirit of Seth or any channeled entities. Also it was unclear why the entity used the synthesizer to say liar; and that the book appeared to be pulled out and beside the book on Seth; although that may be an accurate statement regarding the spirit Seth.

There were many emanations from the voice synthesizer throughout their investigation. I never received a report about their findings and am unsure how I feel about this investigation. However, this group's focus is on tracking ghosts; mine was to better understand the paranormal activity here, and what it might be trying to say about this place and its history, and because of my natural born curiosity.

In recent years the paranormal activity has decreased and seems more deeply ethereal to me. These experiences register more in my unconscious mind, not in physical reality as they had seemingly been doing.

An exception was the time between first contacting P.R.I.ME to suggest they investigate here, and the date of their first investigation, a few things occurred. One was that I felt the entity was agitated; it went back and forth in my mindscape. It is difficult to describe a consciousness of otherness. It feels as if an entity pulled my conscious mind out of me toward their energy. Also there had been some light sparks.

My cat, Orgone, had been acting strangely too. He would be on the couch with me and get down, go across the room and stand at attention looking into the hall and stairway to the bedrooms upstairs and "bad door" room. This went on for about a month. Orgone would stand at the door from this front room to the hall, front door and stairs. He would look up the stairs in a crouching way. He crept in a stalking manner to the hall and stairs. Orgone appeared to be frightened. After the investigation this stopped. I have enjoyed living here in Ripley. Rudy died on February 19, 2013. If there are ghosts here, or not, I am now part of the history of this place too. If anything, these kinds of experiences have allowed me to feel more connected to the spiritual world, of which this physical one is made, and I am still looking for the "gold!"

MARYLAND

AS TOLD BY: MEGAN RIVERA

In 2007 for a roughly three years I lived in Box Hill South in Harford County, Maryland with my family. I was seven years old when we moved in. Our home was on a street called Rock Creek Court.

It was cozy but my sister and I always felt a hint of discomfort while living there. It was just cold all the time. After setting the place up and getting settled in we started experiencing things. Since I was a baby I've been told I've pointed at things that weren't there so it wasn't a brand new experience for me with the paranormal.

On Rock Creek Court in our new home I would be lying in bed at night and looking out into the hallway I would see lantern-like lights bouncing as though they were being carried down the hallway. My sister would wake up to mysterious hand prints on her clothes the size of a man's hand dipped in some sort of residue. She always slept with her bedroom door locked so no one could have gotten in there to do it.

Sometimes when we were home by ourselves and she would be babysitting me we would hear scratching coming from behind the basement door.

Neither of us ever wanted to go into the basement just because the vibe was even creepier down there.

The strangest thing, however, had to be the morning I woke up and headed downstairs to leave for school. I was walking down the stairs and looking over the railing you would clearly be able to see the kitchen.

When I was heading down the stairs I just happened to look into the kitchen where I saw someone kneeling on the floor. They weren't dressed like in modern attire but more-so dressed in rags. As soon as I noticed the person I froze and she looked up at me. It was a heavy set black woman scrubbing something on the tile floor. As I backed away I could see that she did not have any legs.

I ran back upstairs and didn't go back down the stairs until my mom would go with me.

MASSACHUSETTS

AS TOLD BY: MARLON ADAMS

My story begins when I was about 15 living in Leeds, Massachusetts with my parents. At the time, my parents owned a large backyard and my mom owned three pet ducks that would roam around foraging for insects. Our neighbors across the street owned a black dog that would sometimes get loose and run into our yard and chase the ducks. In response, the ducks would run to the driveway of our yard and hide underneath one of the parked cars where the dog couldn't get to them. This was more of a nuisance to us (and the ducks) than anything else, but it was still annoying, as we were all very fond of the ducks and worried that the dog might try to hurt them.

On the day in question, it was a Saturday morning and I was in my room somewhere between the halfway point of just waking up and still coming out of sleep when I heard the familiar panicked 'quacking' of the ducks outside. I knew the sound meant that the ducks were afraid of something, and when I heard the jingling of a collar tag, I knew that the dog from across the street was loose and chasing them again. For some reason this aroused a sense of injustice in me, and I sprang out of bed in nothing but my underwear and angrily headed down the stairs. I walked into the living room, past my parents, my dad was sitting in his usual reclining chair watching television and my mom was positioned on a rubber mat performing her morning aerobics routine. I passed by them without saying anything, and they didn't say anything to me.

I grabbed the first object I laid eyes on to throw at the dog to scare him away, which in this case happened to be a 9-volt battery, laying on the kitchen table just before I reached the front door. I figured it was just heavy enough to get some momentum going and cause some damage.

As I opened the door, one of the ducks came out from under the car in the driveway and gave a prolonged 'quack', which is supposed to be a form of greeting in duck-speak, almost as if to say 'thank god you're here!'. Sure enough, I spotted the dog nearby and hurled the 9-volt at him, and he retreated back across the street. I walked back upstairs to my room, once again passing my parents without saying anything to them or them to me. I feel back into my bed and into sleep.

I later awoke to the sound of my mother's voice as she poked her head in through my bedroom door. "Good morning", she said in her usual cheerful voice.

"Good morning", I said groggily. "I saved your ducks", I added.

"What do you mean?" she asked.

"Oh, that stupid dog from across the street was out there again chasing them and I went outside and shooed him away".

"When did this happen?"

"This morning".

"This morning, are you sure about that?"

"Yeah, I'm sure."

She chuckled. "Honey, I think you were dreaming, your dad and I have been downstairs all morning, we haven't see you once".

Odd, I thought.

"What are you talking about, I walked right past you guys", I said incredulously.

"Okay, what were we doing?", she asked skeptically.

"You were doing your aerobics routine…"

"Yeah…"

"And dad was sitting in his reclining chair…"

"Yeah. Did we say anything to you?"

"No, I just walked past you".

"Well, yeah that's true, but Marlon we've been downstairs all morning and this is the first I've seen you. I'm sorry but I think you dreamed all that".

"No way", I said in disbelief. I got out of bed rethinking what happened and could not believe that it was dream. Surely they just didn't notice me. Although it did seem odd that I would come walking down in my underwear and for them to not say anything. Furthermore, although I have certainly had my share of lucid dreams in my life, I have never woken up and been unable to distinguish a dream from a real memory. Even if I truly believed the dream was really happening at the time of having it, I have never woken up and still thought that it actually happened.

In total disbelief I got dressed and went outside to look for evidence. The first thing I noticed was that the ducks had soot on their backs, which meant that they had in fact been hiding under the truck recently. Still, I could have just heard the sound of them quacking from my room and then dreamt that I got up and went outside. But then as I walked out into the driveway I found, lying on the ground, the 9v battery that I had supposedly thrown. Maybe it could have just been a random battery that happened to be lying out there? And maybe my parents just happened to somehow not notice me coming downstairs first thing in the morning in my underwear and then going back up without any explanation. Maybe...

Now, if someone had told me my dad had not noticed me walk by, I might believe it, as he sometimes gets very absorbed in his television. My mom on the other hand, is a very sharp observer, and I would have a very hard time believing that she didn't notice her oldest son walk right by her twice without saying anything. The obvious explanation is that I dreamt it, somehow couldn't tell that it wasn't real, and then certain physical elements of the external world coincided with the events of my dream. That's plausible right? Maybe not. I am certainly not a religious person by any means, but an experience like this is enough to make me second guess the belief that the material world is all there is and there is no such thing like the soul or the spirit – certainly not one that can leave the physical body and began moving 9-volt batteries around, right?

MICHIGAN

AS TOLD BY: DAVID WAK

I once rented an apartment in old Victorian house on White Street in the south side of Port Huron, Michigan, a town with many reported hauntings. Having grown up and spent half my life there I will attest that while the town is pleasant in some aspects, with a beautiful lake, shore line, and many wonderful natural areas north and west, there was something amiss about the place. There's a certain vibe there that seemed to tell people not to rise above or they might lose their heads. To this day I cannot tell if it was just the collective consciousness of the people, who tended to be a close-minded and provincial bunch, or if there was something else lurking that one could not see except for a glimpse out of the corner of ones eye on occasion. The town certainly seemed ripe for ghosts as it was often a place of waylaid dreams and it's possible there are a lot of unhappy souls up there who refuse to move on.

When I first moved in, the place struck me as strange and somewhat gloomy. It was a second floor apartment with brown wood paneling (talk about gloomy) and brown furniture, but it was cheap and within walking distance of work. It had a narrow, twisting staircase and next to the entrance was another door that led up to the attic. In the attic on the east side you could open a window and hang out on the roof, on the west side there was a door that led to the rest of the attic.

When I checked out the attic, it was a strange set up. There were partially constructed walls as if someone was trying to build a living space up there. What was really weird was there was a new cedar-lined closet space on the south side, in perfect shape and apparently unused. I wondered why someone would go through the trouble of putting that in such an out-of-the-way location. Overall I felt weird vibes up there, although I couldn't put my finger on it. Once, my sister and niece stopped by and I showed them the attic. They both claim to sense the supernatural, something I feel I also have albeit it's much milder in my case. They said they felt a presence and a cold spot near the doorway to the rest of the attic. That made me feel a little nervous at the time but I soon forgot about it. There seemed to be nothing overly strange about the place except for it being a gloomy old apartment.

One time, my landlord came by to do some minor repairs and we talked. I asked him about the attic. When he asked me if I had been up there, he told me not to venture there anymore as the floor was dangerous and he was afraid I might hurt myself and leave him open for a lawsuit. He put a lock on the door soon after. I asked him about the construction up there and he said some previous tenants, whom he described as weird hippie types, had done it and one of them had been trying to build an extra apartment up there without permission (I don't recall if he owned the place then or it they lived there under the previous landlord).

Anyway, in the winter of 1989, my pals Steve and Randy came by to watch the Super Bowl with me. They were getting a little drunk but by that time I was through with drinking, having suffered a bout with Hepatitis A, the year before, while living there (I actually lived at my parents' place for a couple of months to recover the previous winter).

I told them about the weird attic and they got curious. When I told them about it being locked, they laughed and said, "No big deal, we got tools in the car, we can just take the hinges off." I agreed and off they went. I was watching them go down the spiral staircase and as soon as they disappeared I heard as clear as day, a voice. Perhaps it was out loud or maybe in my head but it simply said "Nooooo!!" It was a deep, throaty masculine voice, hoarse like someone with a dry throat or perhaps a longtime smoker. It was both threatening and threatened, like it really didn't want anyone to go up in that attic. I was of course startled and a bit scared but part of me thought, "Hey, fuck you. I live here, I'm paying rent, you're dead, you have little say in the matter." I know it sounds cocky but that's truly how I reacted. I have always had some belief in ghosts; it might be because I come from superstitious people, with my mom being part Irish and my dad being 100 percent Lithuanian. I don't know if that has any bearing, but neither of them dismissed the idea of ghosts. I also believe that with some people, whether here in body or just in spirit, are bullies and if you show them weakness or fear they will exploit that.

Anyway, I didn't tell my friends about it until later on. They came back up and opened up the door and we explored the attic. They agreed it was a strange and somewhat creepy place with the partially built walls and the unused cedar closet. When I told my friend Steve about the incident later he wasn't surprised. He said he also felt something in the apartment and especially the attic and suggested I stay out of there.

I never had another incident there but did have an interesting false alarm once. I was taking a nap after work then woke up to see and feel the end of my bed shaking and vibrating. After the first incident I was freaked out a bit plus very disoriented upon wakening. I turned on the light (it was winter and dark by then) and then turned the radio on to dispel the feeling of being alone with whatever might have been there. I immediately heard a news flash about a small earthquake near Montreal that had a 600-mile radius. That solved the riddle of the shaking bed it seemed.

There was another strange aside to this tale. When I had moved into this apartment, I hadn't seen my folks in a while. When I got around to visiting them, I told my dad where I had moved and he went, "Is it on the second floor, with winding staircase?" I was like, "Dad, how do you know this?" He answered, "Me and your mother lived there when we first got married," and added in his typical droll way, "It's haunted you know." I asked him more and he recalled refrigerator doors being pulled open and slammed shut when no one else was around. I also had another friend who knew a couple that lived there that claimed to have seen a rocking chair rocking by itself.

Later on after I had moved, me and my pal Steve were talking about the place and my incident. He, being more spiritually aware than most, said perhaps the place was infested by an angry spirit, maybe even some sort of minor league demon. He wondered if that contributed to my sickness with Hepatitis A. It never occurred to me to put the two together, but in retrospect I have to wonder. When I got sick, I wasn't sure what was wrong with me except for the fact I couldn't keep food down and was slowly turning yellow. I knew this much - I could hear the reaper coming down the hall for me so to speak and I often slept for 16 hours at a time. I remember troubled dreams although I can't recall what they were about. But now I wonder, did some evil entity that dwelled there cause me to become sick? Did it want me to die there in that gloomy place and perhaps join it in the afterlife?

I do not know. What I do know is I felt more lighthearted when I moved out of there. Sometimes when I'm in Port Huron, I drive past the place and look away. However, I once got out of my car, looked at the place and took some pictures and believe I felt something malicious up in that house lurking behind dirty old curtains. Perhaps it remembered me, and maybe it even wanted another shot at me. Whatever the truth is I'm damn glad to have gotten away from there and whatever might be up there still.

Years after the incident my friend Steve recalled a disturbing detail to this story that I cannot recall at all. He said when we were up in the attic, he saw childlike drawings of flowers on the walls of the cedar closet and speculated that maybe some poor kid was locked up there. I don't know about that but the idea of it makes the tale even more creepy in my mind, when he told me about it I got shivers.

MINNESOTA

AS TOLD BY: Mercedes Tenter

I was always really close to my grandfather. When I was younger, he would play his accordion for me, or have me on his lap while he played his organ. More than once, he had looked into my eyes and told me how beautiful I was, while his eyes filled with tears. So, you can understand that when he passed away in 2008 from Alzheimer's disease, I was heartbroken.

I remember a day or two after his death; my grandmother asked if my mother and I would come over to help her go through picture albums to find pictures of my grandfather to display at the funeral. It was a very solemn experience. We discussed our fond memories of him while shifting through picture after picture, picking the ones we thought best showed his personality, including some of him and I.

There was a point during the process of sifting through memories that I was feeling especially calm. I remember just sitting there, listening to my grandmother and my mother talk. I guess you could say I was feeling 'at peace'. As I sat, really not thinking or feeling anything, something out of the corner of my eye made me turn my head towards the sliding glass door that lead to the deck. At this point, it was fairly dark outside, and there was nobody at the house except us three. Yet, I saw something that evening that I still can't explain.

Everything happened in a matter of seconds, and the whole time I was feeling especially somber and was hardly even thinking. I saw something in that glass sliding door that looked like what I can only describe as a thick wisp of white smoke. I remember my brain calculating, in those few short moments, trying to come up with a conclusion for what this was, and I came up with, "reflection". My grandma smokes, so my immediate thought was that I had to be seeing a reflection of a wisp of her smoke. So I slowly turned my head, still rather out of sorts, and looked to where it should be in the room.

I can still remember the image of the top of the refrigerator where I had stared for about five seconds. Whatever had made that reflection should have been directly in front of the refrigerator, very near to the ceiling. Yet what I saw... was absolutely nothing. I then noticed that there was also a fan in the kitchen, blowing in that direction. And my brain was telling me that this made no sense it all. The smoky-like image I saw was moving gently, slowly. And if there was any smoke in that area, the fan would have blown it so fast I probably wouldn't have seen it at all. And do you want to know the strangest part? My grandma did not have a cigarette lit at that moment.

The back of my neck tingled as I considered the possibility that what I saw was probably outside. But I was still so oddly calm, that I totally disregarded everything. And didn't think about it until later when my mother and I got home.

Later that evening, my mother and I got home and were chatting about how it all went at my grandmas. She was joking about how it was funny nothing 'creepy' or 'spiritual' had happened, since my grandma is always seeing things and having experiences. That's when I brought up what I had seen. I kind of thought nothing of it since I'm sort of a non-believer when it comes to ghosts. But after telling the story to my mom, she immediately went upstairs and e-mailed my grandma the story I told. My mom told me, that it was definitely possible that since my grandfather and I were so close, maybe he had tried to show himself to me, to possibly say goodbye. And that could have been why I felt so immensely content and at peace.

I started to tear-up. Her explanation hit home in a way I didn't think it would, especially since I don't believe in spiritual things like this. It just made sense to me, in a way. And now I'm not so sure that I don't believe.

MISSISSIPPI

AS TOLD BY: KIMBERLY DAVIS

It all started when I was 9 and I fell out of a tree one afternoon while playing around at my childhood home.

Later that night, my mom, my sister, and I were sitting down having dinner and I let her know that I fell out the tree. She told me that I was a tough cookie because I didn't hurt myself falling from the tree.

I got up from the table and headed to the kitchen to wash my plate and as I was about to put my plate on the table there was a glow coming from the window. I looked and was shocked to see a glowing man; he was all gold and it looked to me as though it was trying to open the window to get in. I stood there for a moment to see what it was doing, and suddenly he looked at me like I scared him and he took off.

I ran to my mom and told her what I had seen but she had a puzzled look on her face like I was crazy. She took me outside to show me there was no way that a glowing man was in the window unless it was seven feet tall. I was surprised that she didn't believe me.

A couple weeks later we went to my grandma's house and my mom was explaining to her why I was upset so I got up and went outside to play in the middle of her telling my grandma what happened.

I was outside playing with my cousin that came to visit and after a while I'd forgotten that I was mad because I was having such a good time. The two of us were racing and I had to stop and catch my breath, looking up into the sky as I do, and what I saw caught me off guard. It was a person but it was all black looking right at me so I yelled and pointed to get my cousin's attention. I wave at the person who was looking at me from the clouds and it waved back.

When I looked at my cousin to see if they'd seen the same thing, they shook their head "no". I was floored because I'm the only one seeing this figure. I stood there questioning my sanity. Then my trance was broken by my mom asking if I was okay.

At this point, my mom took me to the doctor to make sure there wasn't something wrong that was causing me to see these things, but all the tests came back perfectly normal.

Twenty-five years later I moved into my first house and had a good feeling, so I was happy. But only a couple weeks later things started to happen, though I wasn't scared.

My first experiences in the house were at night, when it would get real cold in certain parts of the house but I brushed it off. Weeks later I started to feel like somebody was watching me though there was no one living in the house but me.

Eventually, I explained what was going on to a neighbor of mine and she suggested that I talk to whoever was in the house. Later that night, I took her advice and I was surprised to find out there was a lady spirit in my house and she was making her presence known.

As time went on, I noticed she didn't like some of my cousins or friends (only males). She started to move or pick up things around the house while they were around. There was no question that she wanted them out. One time I had a couple of people over and we were sitting in the living room talking. I was looking at the TV when suddenly everything got quiet. I didn't think much of it until my cousin hit me on the legs and started calling my name to turn and look. By the time I turned to look, everybody had a crazy look on their face.

My friend says the cigarette in the ashtray floated up into the air, turned sideways, then dropped back down in the ashtray. I couldn't say anything for a minute and some of my company got up and left.

Later that night I put my phone on the table so I could record the spirit in my home. I was surprised to catch an EVP and some pictures of the spirit.

The last big event was when I was going out of town with a couple of friends. I went to my neighbor to inform her that I'd be gone and asked if she would watch my house. She told me not to worry and that she'd watch the house.

Later on that night, she called me and said, "Don't be alarmed but the lights on your house are coming on and off by themselves." I asked her if she thought someone had broken into my house, but she said no, that everything was good. When I got back in town, everybody that lives on the street had seen what was happening and that a lady was even seen standing in my window. I was floored by what they were telling me.

People stopped coming to my house due to these paranormal events taking place.

MISSOURI

AS TOLD BY: Rick Fogle

When I was a kid we lived in the old Governor's Mansion in Carrollton, Missouri.

I remember very little about the house but for a few things. The house was so big my older brothers and sister would ride their bikes inside the house. It had huge three story pillars that went around the front and the right side of the house. There were huge acorn trees around the whole house.

When we first moved into the house I quickly gained an imaginary friend as most kids do. My imaginary friend's name was John Alfred.

Not long after we moved into the house, my dad, who was in the Navy, was on active duty at sea. It was just my mom and us kids.

Mom would hear many strange noises in the house one of which I do remember. A loud banging noise from the third floor attic that shook the whole house.

It would happen late at night but not every night. My two uncles Pat and Dave came over to the house one night and it happened while they were there. I remember well sitting on the steps, playing with one of those things you could cook plastic and melt it into little animal shapes. They went running upstairs and the noise stopped before they got up there. On the third floor, there were two huge old oak doors from the original entrance to the house. Both of my uncles were able to lift up one side of the old door and drop it. It was so heavy they could only lift it up a little way. They were big guys at the time and in shape as well. My mom said it was the sound but nowhere near as loud as before. There was absolutely no one up there and no way for anyone to have hidden, as the room on the third floor was completely open.

There were many other occurrences at this house that I do not remember.

The thing I do remember is when I was in kindergarten. We were taking tests one day and were out at recess. My friend and I did not want to come in. Finally, I told him we were going to be in trouble if the teacher kept calling. He said fine but he wasn't coming in. I remember him well: I could tell you exactly what he was wearing, what he looked like, and the tone of his voice. I remember looking back at him wondering why he got to stay outside and I didn't. A few days later, the teacher spoke to my mom about how I was misbehaving that day. She told my mom I was the last one to come in; there was no one else out there but me.

I haven't seen anything since nor do I want to, and I have to say I don't remember ever being scared around then either. When my dad got back from being at sea we moved away. As we were driving away from the house I apparently opened the car door while we were driving away on the interstate. I said my friend John Alfred wasn't coming with us. Apparently my dad gave my mom a look like "what the heck is wrong with that one?"

We have done extensive research on the Internet trying to find out if a John Alfred ever lived in the house. It was not a child of the Governor, but a family before him. John Alfred died of polio in that house. He was a child... could not find an exact age on him though. There's no way we would have even known his name back then for me to have picked it up as a little kid.

MONTANA

AS TOLD BY: WINTER MYST

I was living in Butte, Montana the winter of 1978. My husband and I had just bought a house on what people call the "flats" and I had just had my second daughter that February. Her room was right next to ours, and my other daughter's room was just down the hall so they were both close by.

I will never forget the spring night when I thought my beautiful baby girl was possessed in Linda Blair fashion. It was a nightmare in reality on some incredibly evil things that lurk on the other side of my world.

I remember sleeping soundly when a noise woke me up. It was the sound of what sounded like maniacal laughter coming from my baby daughter's room. I sat straight up as I listened to this horrible laughter. Not only was it coming from her room, but it sounded like it was coming from her. "Oh my God!" I thought, "What is happening to my baby?"

My heart was pounding and my body shaking as I threw the covers back and jumped out of bed. I was planning on running into her room grabbing her and then grabbing my other daughter on the way out the door. Unlike some television shows or movies today, I did not plan on waiting around to see what it was. I just wanted to grab my babies and run.

As I put both my feet on the floor, something picked me up off the floor and slammed me back down on the bed. It didn't hurt me, but whatever it was wasn't going to let me get by. Two more times, as I tried to get up, whatever this thing was picked me up and threw me down on the bed. Finally, on the fourth try, I was able to run from it.

Instead of running into my daughter's room, I ran into the living room. I immediately noticed that my lamps were on, the lamp shades were twirling, that laughing was loud and crazy sounding and there seemed to be some kind of weird language written on the bottom of both of my lamp shades as they continued to spin.

I did the only thing I could think of. I immediately dropped to my knees, put my hands over my ears, closed my eyes and with fear touching my soul said, "Oh God, My God! Please make it stop!"

As soon as the words were out of my mouth, everything was quiet. The laughter was gone, the lamp shades had stopped twirling but the lights stayed on and the writing was gone. I could only kneel there for several minutes, my entire body shaking, and my heart beating at Mach one.

I knew I had to go into my baby's room, I was so very frightened. I couldn't help but imagine walking into her room and seeing her floating above her bed, eyes glowing red and her head twist around her body Linda Blair style as that maniacal laugh comes out of her body. I was so scared. I finally took a deep breath and slowly got to my feet.

My entire body was trembling as I slowly walked to her room, praying to God the entire time that she would be okay. My legs were weak and I actually got dizzy as I slowly opened her door. Well, no floating baby so that was a good sign. I walked over to her crib and she was sound asleep. You could tell her covers hadn't been messed with and that she was sleeping sound. It looked as if nothing disturbing had happened to her. I thanked God with all my heart that she was safe. I bent down and kissed her cheek, she smiled that angelic smile all babies seem to have. She seemed content in her little world. Like Angels were watching over her, and more than likely they truly were on this night.

To this day I have no idea why that happened. Some people can think it was a nightmare or my imagination. In all my life I can promise you, I have never been picked up and literally, physically thrown down before or since that happened. I know it happened and that is all that matters.

NEBRASKA

AS TOLD BY: ANONYMOUS

These events occurred in the 1980s, when I was living in Omaha, Nebraska.

I bought a house in Omaha, and lived there for two years. The house was built in 1929 and was in need of various repairs, so I got a great deal on a Contract for Deed.

A few weeks after moving in, objects began to appear on the kitchen floor, in the same corner. First, an antique pepper shaker, half-full of old pepper. Then an antique crochet hook and a slip of very old paper with some unintelligible scrawling. None of these items belonged to me.

I would then begin to hear footsteps on the ceiling of the living room, as if someone lived upstairs, but that part of the home was one-story (the master bedroom was upstairs in a separate portion of the home).

Later, the scent of a sweaty man would wake me up in the middle of the night, but I never saw an apparition.

One day, I was coming home from work and unlocked the deadbolt lock to the front door. It was the original door from 1929, and also had the original skeleton key-type lock, which never worked. However, the door wouldn't open. I checked for anything that would be stuck around the door, I also unscrewed the faceplate from the deadbolt and saw the deadbolt mechanism was normal. The bolt was retracted, it was perfectly unlocked even still, the door would not budge.

I finally retrieved a ladder from the back yard, remembering that I'd left the upstairs bedroom window open, and climbed in through the window. I went down to the front door & tried to open it from the inside - it still wouldn't move. I unscrewed the faceplate of the skeleton-type doorknob/lock and removed it. Inside I found a spent .22 caliber shell inside, jamming the antique locking mechanism into the lock position.

I calmly replaced the faceplate and doorknob, and the door then opened easily.

I turned to go from the living room toward the kitchen, and noticed on the hardwood flooring a large, dark stain that hadn't been there before. It seemed to be slowly spreading, but was imbedded into the wood. I figured this was something to do with the spirit that was inhabiting the house, so I went to my next-door neighbor's home to casually ask what she knew about the previous owner. Luckily she was an elderly lady who had lived there since the 1950s and told me a story that sent chills down my spine.

I learned that the previous owner was a small-time whiskey runner during Prohibition, a chronic alcoholic, living there alone. He suffered from depression, and sometime around 1965, had committed suicide. He did so in the living room putting a .22 caliber pistol to his head...

I ultimately signed the property back to the realty company and moved to Minnesota.

NEVADA

AS TOLD BY: LIZ HARRINGTON

Back in April of 1987 I was 21 years old getting off the late shift at a local diner I worked at. My apartment was about 20 miles outside Reno, so I had a way to go on my way home. I remember clocking out a little after 2 a.m. and getting in my car to head home. It was just like any other night, I was tired and smelled like burgers and fries. All I wanted to do was be away from people, take a shower, and go to sleep.

I couldn't have been in the car more than 15 minutes when I started to feel really strange. It was almost as if someone had drugged me; I went into a strange haze. All of the sudden I felt very sick like I was going to vomit, so I pulled over to the side of the road, got out of the car and puked.

After that the strangest thing happened, I get back in the car to look at the clock and it said it was 4:12 a.m. I had only stepped out of the car for a couple of minutes there was no possible way it could be 4:12 a.m. Back then we didn't have cell phones, so I kept driving home to check my alarm clock just to be sure I wasn't going mad. By the time I got home my alarm clock and stove clock both read 4:30. It was so bizarre and strange. I showered, got in my pajamas, and went to sleep.

I will never forget the dreams I had that night - they were so vivid. I was puking on the side of the road when these two creatures a little under five feet tall with long faces came walking up to me. Frightened, I began to run but then started feeling dizzy and I remember falling.

The next thing I know they are carrying me by my arms and legs. After that they are stripping me out of my uniform and putting me on this ice cold table where there are about ten of these alien creatures surrounding me. It wasn't like in the movies where they were poking and probing you but they were definitely violating me. They were very fascinated with my feet and my belly button but touched me almost every other place you can think of.

I felt way too exhausted to fight back so I just let them do what they had to do. The last thing I remember them doing is putting this very small metal looking object in my ear and then taking it out. I woke up instantly after that still in my bed. The weird thing was it was only 5:15 so I had only been "asleep" about 20 minutes.

I haven't shared this experience with many people because I don't want anyone to think I'm crazy, but I know for a fact that I'm not crazy. These events cannot be explained, but I hope one day I can find answers to the questions about what really happened that night.

NEW HAMPSHIRE

AS TOLD BY: DANIEL PEGG

In the fall of 2007, I was attending a now defunct liberal arts college located in southern New Hampshire. A strictly enforced dry campus set in a tiny rural town had its limitations for entertaining a bunch of young college kids. Many of us were left to our own devices for fun in between classes, which usually involved getting stoned and wandering through some of the nearby wooded trails. One could get a sense that the area's bucolic beauty had not changed much in the last couple centuries, even the buildings on campus consisted of pre- Revolutionary War barns and rambling colonial houses. The buildings all had their own individual alleged story. One of these buildings produced a narrative that took place during a harsh winter in the 1800's, when an isolated, grief-stricken farmer shot and killed his sickly wife and children before himself, rather than to see them painfully waste away in a smallpox epidemic. Of course, these stories were all entirely undocumented. Although there were old bullet holes in some of the interior paneling that no one alive could explain.

Typical of old New England settlements, the local cemetery was a stone walled off section of field across the street from a white paneled church. This graveyard quickly became a source of interest, as it was a space we had to cut through to get to some our more regularly walked route in the bordering woods. The cemetery was unique in that some of the older headstones were carved with varying cherubic facial expressions on them. Some of the stone angel faces appeared grimacing while others were clearly smiling. It was debated as to whether these faces were hints at the spiritual fate of the deceased as judged by a bitter headstone mason, or if there was even any intention at all. Either way, the old cemetery mixed with the unaccounted legends seemed evident that the sleepy little town had a very tangible and seemingly dark past.

One night about a week before Halloween, a handful of us were sitting outside in front of the dorms, smoking bummed cigarettes and complaining about the usual boredom. Someone in the group came up with the idea to visit the graveyard that night. Practice some amateur "ghost hunting" with digital sound recorders in hand. Mimicking some televised mainstream paranormal investigative show, someone grabbed their own digital recorder while a couple others decided to use their cell phones as recording devices. Then we all made our way up the road to the leafless tree lined burial ground.

Walking through the cemetery at night had an entire different feel than during the day. There was a sort of heaviness in the air as we all stealthy climbed over the wall to avoid the locked iron gate. "Jen," was the more confident in communicating with the dead. She was brazen enough to ask questions into the air: "What is your name?" "How did you die?" "When did you die?" Those sort of things. Although Jen admitted that we may not get an answer to the question, it would probably evoke some kind of a guttural response, if anything. She said that ghosts liked to be treated respectfully and she made sure to politely say "Thank you," and "Goodbye" after her momentary pauses in between questions.

We trudged along in a huddled group, our feet crunching against the autumn debris. It was made sure that any noise, even a stick snapping underfoot, was audibly recorded as being such. We made a point to stop in front of the gathering of the angel face stones, and the series of questions were repeated. Although we made sure to emphasize silence in between questions, one of the more skeptical ones, "Marie," exclaimed that her cell phone video had caught an "orb," this floating ball of light, just overhead of us during the questioning. Weirdly, this ball of orange light was only visible through the cell phone screen. At one point, a headlight from a passing car in the distance came into view, showing that the source of the light was not from anything that we could see in our immediate environment. We wandered along further into the graveyard. There was a sense of unease as we walked farther away from the street. It was a feeling of being invasive, uninvited, images of people crawling across the ground towards us seemed to come into my mind as stopped here and there to continue recording. Jen, with her more professional approach, reminded us that it was unwise to listen to the recordings while we were still on the "hunt" and that it was best to wait until we returned to the safety of the campus. It was then that we realized Marie, with her recorded orb, was missing from the group.

Someone tried phoning her, no answer. After calling out her name a few times we decided to press on. We stopped intuitively at the base of a large old tree, and sat gathered around in a circle. The questions were repeated, and this time answered more audibly without the aid of a device. A low whistling sound seemed to emerge out of nowhere, while thudding sounds against the ground sporadically were heard surrounding us. It almost felt as though people, perhaps children, were jumping from the gnarly overhead branches to see what we were doing. It was then we all felt as though we had put in our time, we thanked "them" and said goodbye.

We found Marie back on campus, visibly shaken up and at the verge of tears. Pulling a couple of us aside she admitted that she had "pissed herself" and resulted in her fleeing from the graveyard. She explained that while the rest of the group moved forward, she stayed behind to record the little ball of light, which appeared to be moving along back and forth for a while. It was then that she felt as though someone had grabbed her arm and pushed her. Urinating herself in fear, she ran away from the graveyard totally aside herself. She rolled up her sleeve to reveal her right arm had visible black and blue bruises making up the shape of a large hand. The impression of big fingernails was embedded into her flesh. That had the most sobering effect on me. This was real. Upon hearing of Marie's experience, we excitedly gathered around Jen's recorder, started from the beginning and pressed Play. At first the recordings were nothing, the sounds of our shuffling feet and the occasional cough were heard. Even the passing car in the distance was heard driving by, but nothing else. During Jen's second round of questions a clearly whispered "repeat the question," seemed to latch on over Jen's words. A lot of excited exclamations arouse from the group, a few awoken students from the told us to shut up in unison from the dorm windows.

As we listed further to the recordings, it sounded as though phone lines had crossed, at time even the person asking the question's voice would suddenly be talked over with garbled static sounds and voices seeming to have a conversation. We wrote down what bits appeared audible to us, at one point a gurgling sounding "Help Me," came through, more terrifying than any horror movie produced soundbite. Phrases such as "He hates her so much," "Come closer" and a child screeching "Daddy" came out from bits of static. One voice simply stating, "He's here," seemed to be directed at me. I was the only male there. I lost a lot of sleep that night.

Days later, Jen received a worried phone call from her parents. They asked her what was wrong, Jen, confused stated that she was fine and asked why they were concerned. They told her that they had just received a mass amount of texts from her number repeating the phrase "help me, help me, help me, help me." Startled, Marie could find no such text message in her Sent folder. It was as if whatever she had recorded in that graveyard had not only followed her home, but had connected itself with her phone.

Word got on throughout the student body about the voice recordings in the graveyard. Even upon hearing it, some didn't believe us. Others made unsuccessful attempts to do what we had achieved. Chalking up more to the disbelief of our brush with the supernatural. But everyone involved knows the truth. Since the closing of the college, the graveyard probably doesn't get the usual round of restless young visitors that it used to. I would like to think whatever lingering spirits were there have moved on. Maybe it was already determined by the expressions of the faces of the stone angels.

NEW JERSEY

AS TOLD BY: Dawn Lisa Cuccinello

August 25, 1989 three young teenagers; Larry, Frank, and my Tommy, partied in the famous Jersey Shore town of Seaside Heights. On their way home into Toms River, New Jersey they had to drive over a bridge, connecting the New Jersey island to the mainland and get back home at their designated times instructed by their parents.

My Tommy wanted to stop in a convenient store on the way home to buy a pack of smokes. Frank walked in with my Tommy while Larry waited in the truck.

Inside of the convenient store Larry's nemesis, Donny, lurked over by my Tommy and Frank. Donny knew full well that Larry must have been waiting outside.

My Tommy and Frank paid for their purchases and walked back to the truck. They got back in with Larry in the driver's seat, my Tommy in the passenger's seat, and Frank in the back.

Larry put the truck in reverse, and backed out of the parking space. He then placed the shaft in drive and went forward onto the busy road.

Out of nowhere, Donny suddenly jumped on the truck while it was in motion, and punched Larry in the face, continuously, through the driver's side window. The truck went out of control, and flipped over. Donny was thrown, limbs went flying everywhere. His leg tossed on someone's front lawn, the other leg was in the road.

Frank went flying through the back windshield, thankfully unharmed he went to get help.

Larry's chest was crushed at the steering wheel and passed away on the way to the hospital.

My Tommy lay crushed under the truck. He was airlifted to the ER and died in the intensive care unit eleven days later from pneumonia.

Two weeks later I was working at Burger King in the Ocean County Mall in Toms River, New Jersey. I was extremely depressed about losing my Tommy and was not quite sure how to handle it. Suddenly, I saw Tommy. He walked into the Burger King with his long black silky hair waving with every strut, wearing a blue flannel shirt and ripped denim jeans. Quickly, he went into the back of the Burger King. I ran after him, but he had vanished.

Concerned for my sanity, I walked back towards the cash register. Two boys that my Tommy and I were acquaintances with, Bobby and Mark, ran into the Burger King towards the back, stopped looked and looked at me. "Dawn," said Bobby, "We just saw Tommy." "What was he wearing?" I asked. "A blue flannel shirt and jeans," said Bobby.

As the years passed that Burger King later got renovated into an Applebee's.

In October of 2010 I dined at that Applebee's with my two-year-old son, Harley. He and I sat against a wall at a small booth. To our left were tables that nestled against a Plexiglas wall that consistently shook, as if someone were punching it. Whenever this occurred all of the wait staff would stop and cringe. "Mama," said Harley during the meal, "The ghost walks very fast." "Okay," I said thinking that he was so cute.

As the waitress brought the check the glass shook once more. I asked her what that was. She said that they aren't sure but the previous night a spirit was caught on their security camera during the night; a spirit with long black hair.

NEW MEXICO

AS TOLD BY: Wayne Lee

The first thing I noticed was her eyes.

It was Friday night October, 1968, early in my sophomore year of college. My housemate Bryce and I were at an underage dance club. The band was a local knock-off of Big Brother and the Holding Company, but without Janis. A light show flooded the walls and ceiling with fluid, amoebic shapes. For some strange reason, Bryce and I hadn't smoked any dope beforehand, and there wasn't any alcohol available, so we were sipping root beers, checking out the girls.

One in particular caught my eye as she swirled around the dance floor. She appeared to be Hispanic, had copper skin and blue-black hair, wore a peasant blouse and floor-length Indian skirt. She was barefoot, moved like the light show, organically, effortlessly as a leaf in the wind. I finally got up the nerve to ask her to dance and she accepted. Her name was Conchita, she said. She had just moved to Bellingham from Pueblo, Colorado, led here by "spirit." I was immediately captured by her eyes, intensely dark, open and smiling, searching deep inside me. We danced together till the place closed at two, then she asked if she could get a ride home.

We dropped her off in front of an apartment building and, instead of trying to kiss her or wrangle an invitation inside, as per usual in that free love era, we left her there drove back to our house. Again, we didn't smoke or drink anything. I told Bryce I couldn't get over Conchita, felt like I had seen her before, or perhaps known her from somewhere in my past, maybe even from a past life. This got us going on a discussion about reincarnation, then the origins of life on Earth, then the possibility of life on other planets. Eventually our "what ifs" led us to parallel universes.

"What if there's another universe just like this one somewhere?" Bryce asked.

"What if there's another planet somewhere in that universe just like this one somewhere?" I replied. Then we really got on a roll.

"What if there are two people on that planet just like you and me?"

"What if those two people are having the exact same conversation we're having right now?"

"What if everything there is exactly the same as it is here, happening at exactly the same time?"

"What if there's an infinite number of other planets where everything is happening the same as here?"

"What if there are an infinite number of souls exactly the same as ours?"

"If that's true, then we're infinite and omnipresent. Does that make us God?"

"Does that make everyone God?"

"Does that mean there is no God?"

My heart was throbbing, my skin tingling, my brain strained by the exertion, trying to imagine the mind-fuckingly infinite number of possibilities. Then, suddenly, I felt something snap inside me.

"What's the matter?" Bryce asked. "You look weird."

"I feel weird. It feels like something just broke in my brain, almost like my mainspring snapped or something."

Bryce tried to pull me out of it by putting on Led Zeppelin's first album. Not only was I not interested in it, I didn't even tap my foot—something I've always done involuntarily to music. I told him to take it off. So he put on another favorite, Judy Collins' "Wildflowers." Again, I told him to shut it off.

"It's weird, Bryce. Music just feels completely foreign to me, like it's nothing. In fact, everything feels foreign. This couch—I don't want to sit on it because it feels unnatural. This room, this house, you, everything just feels so—like I'm not part of it at all."

I sat on the floor, but didn't feel comfortable there, either. By now Bryce was a little freaked out. "What do you think it could be?"

"I don't know, but I know what it's not. It's not an acid flashback. It's not a dream. It's much more real than that. I just feel...like a completely different person, not like myself at all. I feel so neutral, like I'm between death and birth or something. Not even of this world. I don't feel nice or friendly or like myself at all—almost kind of violent. No, not really violent, just capable of violence, like an animal or a cave man or something."

"You wanta throw some darts?"

I stared at Bryce, saw fear in his eyes. "I better not. I might throw them at you. I feel like I could kill you right now and not think twice about it."

"Why don't you sit down, Wayne. I'll make you some tea...."

"I don't want to sit down. I need to move. I'm gonna take a walk. If I step in front of a car or get killed or kill someone else, don't worry about it. It's just what has to happen."

"Wayne—"

But I was out the front door and gone into the night.

I started walking, kind of slumping and huffing like a beast. My cheeks hung limply and I felt like I had almost a scowl on my face. I had no idea where I was going. Then I looked up and saw the apartment building where I'd dropped Conchita off. It was now three o'clock, but time didn't matter to me. I walked in the front door, up the stairs and down the hall. When I came to room #3, I stopped, turned the doorknob and walked in. She hadn't told me her apartment number, but somehow I knew that was it. There, sitting cross-legged on the floor in the middle of the living room, surrounded by candles, was Conchita.

"I've been waiting for you," she said calmly.

I sat opposite her and told her all that had happened over the past hour. She didn't look surprised, didn't interrupt, just listened.

"Wow—I didn't know that happened to anyone else!" she said, her eyes lighting up. "That's happened to me a whole bunch of times!"

I told her I needed to keep moving and she said she'd come with me. So we went walking with no destination in mind. I found a 3-foot piece of scrap iron and picked it up, banged it against street signs and telephone poles as we passed them. "If anyone tries to hurt you, I'll kill them," I said, deadly serious.

We walked for about an hour through the abandoned downtown streets. Conchita told me she was a witch, a good witch, that she had powers. "I made you come to me," she said, taking my hand. When we got back to her place, she asked me if I wanted to come up. Normally, I would not have refused such an offer, but I told her I had to keep walking.

I took off again, not having any idea where I was going, not caring. Carrying my iron club, on the lookout for enemies, for danger. Then I stopped and looked up and realized I was in front of the house where three girls I knew lived. They were not close friends, but for some reason I knew I needed to talk to them. It was now four o'clock, but their lights were on. Without knocking, I walked in the front door. They were sitting at the dining room table, throwing yarrow stalks, consulting the I Ching. I sat at the table and told them what had happened that night.

"Let's see what the oracle says," Kajita said.

So I went through the half-hour ritual of throwing the stalks. When we found out my hexagram, she read the text—the description, judgment, image, explanation of the placement of all six lines. When she finished, we all discussed the meaning, and they all agreed on an interpretation of the reading was almost word for word what I had told Bryce and Conchita earlier that night: that I was between death and birth.

They were concerned about me, asked if I wanted to crash on their couch. I didn't even bother to thank them for the offer, or the reading or the tea—politeness was not part of my emotional makeup just then—but said I had to keep walking.

I got home about six, just as the sun was starting to rise. I still felt like a cave man, physical, almost brutal. Definitely not myself. But I lay down on my mattress on the floor, still fully dressed, still holding my weapon, and managed to get some sleep. When I awoke a few hours later—having overslept my nine o'clock English lit class, I was once again myself. But the night's bizarre happenings were still vivid in my mind, and remain so to this day.

Whatever the explanation of the event is—whether I was possessed, had a psychotic break, some kind of spiritual rebirth or whatever—doesn't really matter. What did—and still does—matter is that it opened my mind and heart to an infinite realm of possibilities. If this could happen to me, I reasoned, then who am I to deny the truth of any kind of spiritual experience that happens to anyone else? How can I claim to know what is real when there are other kinds of reality out there that are beyond my own limited experience, understanding and even imagination? There's more to life than just what we can see, hear, feel, I thought. There absolutely some kind of spirit world out there, and I want to find out more.

Oh, by the way, Conchita moved in with me the next week. We lived together for six months, until spirit moved her and her backpack to the nearest I-5 on-ramp, where she stuck out her thumb and disappeared from my life.

NEW YORK

AS TOLD BY: Lita Benson

I was an active theater arts student at Hartwick College in Oneonta, New York and most theater people have a fascination with ghosts.

Our theater ghost was affectionately called Fred because no one truly knew what his name was and so the name "Fred" stuck.

Being a college student I had bouts of procrastination and one day I needed to finish a project for one of my theater classes. Around 6:30-7:00 a.m., I was by myself in the Black Box Theater workshop, listening to my Jersey Boys soundtrack on my laptop and trying to finish my scale model that was due at 10:00 a.m.

I was about halfway through my project when the song "Walk Like A Man" came on. As I was hot gluing one of my background pieces to my model I heard footsteps in our props loft that was right above me. I looked up and didn't see anyone. I dropped my glue gun and quickly walked over to our Green Room which was around the corner from the workshop. My heart was racing and I was breathing heavy. I tried calming myself down, saying things like "It's just

Fred and he's just saying hi. It's okay, just focus on your project."

After a couple of minutes, I finally composed myself and walked back over to the workbench where my project and laptop were. Another few minutes went by and I was deep into my project. The song "Cry For Me" came on and there's a line in the song that says "Well, you had your fun, Don't go baby, With someone new, Don't go baby..." After the second "Don't go baby" I heard the footsteps again up in the props loft, and this time it was louder than before.

I pulled the hot glue plug out of the outlet, left my laptop and my project on the workbench, and bolted out of the Black Box Theater.

NORTH CAROLINA

AS TOLD BY: ANONYMOUS

I was raised by my mother and grandmother. North Carolina is home to me, although we had moved around a lot when I was younger, along with my cousin whom my grandmother had attained custody of. We consider ourselves sisters.

When I was a girl, my mother, who will always be a workaholic, got financing on a brand new trailer and put it on a few acres of land. We were so excited. Suddenly, and as strange as it may seem, because the trailer was brand new, strange things started happening. It wasn't the first time I had dealt with the paranormal, but it was the first time I had encountered very negative spirits.

I remember several occasions when they would leave us alone at the house just long enough to run to the store or something.

We would be talking and goofing off, doing what kids do, when we started hearing what sounded like my mom's full size van pull in the driveway.

We heard two doors shut and what sounded like my mother and grandmother getting out of the van and talking while doing so, we heard this talking all the way up to the door, what we never could figure out though, is what the voices were saying. They always seemed so muffled. It WAS their voices though.

The very first time this happened, we were excited that they were back, hoping they brought junk food in hand. My sister and I ran to the door, there was no doubt in our minds that they were back.

Problem was as soon as the door opened, the voices stopped, it would become an eerie dead silence.

No one was at the neighbors house...

No cars in the driveway.

When this happened, NO ONE seemed to be around.

This happened on and off the entire time we lived there.

We felt like we were being watched almost constantly.

One night, I got up to use the restroom, our room was at the end so we had to walk through the house to get to it. I had never been scared of the dark before so I never turned on the lights, normally the moon was bright enough to light up the trailer as there was only a couple trees in the yard.

So there I was half asleep and sitting on the toilet relieving myself, when I suddenly felt I was being watched. The hairs on the back of my neck stood up and at that same moment, I was watching what was watching me! A tall, dark, thin shadow of a person was standing in the shower. I seen all of it, hands, arms, legs, head, neck... it was right there! There just wasn't any features. It was so still... I could feel very negative energy. I yanked up my pants and ran as fast as I could back through the house, as I was running I heard something that scares the life out of me to this day, IT WAS LAUGHING AT ME. Maybe because I was trying to run away from it. Maybe it liked scaring people. I ran in my bedroom and threw the covers over my head. I was terrified.

Now, this story scares me, and I don't tell very many people about it.

But the questions I ask myself scare me even more.

My grandmothers bed was right next to the bathroom. I always woke her up for comfort if something was wrong or I'd had a bad dream... but that night I didn't. Why?

Also, it never even crossed my mind to turn on the bathroom light, but what would I have seen if I had? Would it have been there still? Would it still have been just a shadow?

My cousin and I walked around that whole development, we made friends with the other kids, we had so many great adventures. We had experiences almost everywhere we went.

On one walk in particular, we weren't very far from the house, I heard chains dragging behind us on the asphalt, the sound was faint at first, and I asked my sister if she'd heard it, she said no so we kept on walking. Well, it kept getting louder and sounded like it was right behind us, she started hearing it too before too long. Her face was pale white and I knew mine had to be also. We mustered all the bravery inside of us and stopped walking, turned around, looked behind us. The noise stopped, everything eerily still and silent. We started walking again, and it started up again. We did this a few times, each time we looked back and stopped walking the sound would stop then start again when we'd continue. Finally, we got spooked and ran home.

We learned later in life that the development, in slavery days, was a southern plantation that had a huge slave population. The slave holders there were some of the worst kind.

Oh, the goose bumps I got when I heard this. You know what though? It all makes sense now, the pieces to the puzzle finally fit, and we now have answers to the questions we had since we were kids.

NORTH DAKOTA

AS TOLD BY: ANONYMOUS

As unbelievable as this may be, my mom was haunted by a demon. My little sister and I did not believe her because this "demon" never bothered us. This seemed to go on for about a month before I knew she was serious.

One early morning around 2:15 a.m. right before my 15th birthday I heard screaming from my mom's room. I jumped out of bed and ran downstairs to see what was going on. By the time I entered her room she stopped panicking, like the demon knew I was coming to save her. My sister trickled in the room shortly after me and turned the lights on.

Shaking she held out her arms to hug us as she was holding back tears, I could tell how frightened she was. As I looked down at her arms she had three very distinct bite marks up and down her arms, it was terrifying. She noticed I had seen them and quickly pulled her sleeves down to make them disappear from my sister's sight. She told me when I opened the door this white light came flooding in the room, as if an angel was watching over her and the demon immediately went away. That night we all slept together hoping that would keep the demon away, and it did.

The next day we called one of our neighbors who was a priest and told him what happened. Although he didn't help us out, he referred us to a friend who came and blessed the house that night. To this day, as far as I know, my mom has never been bothered again.

OHIO

AS TOLD BY: Sarah Thompson

My story starts in my teens. My sister and I always felt that our childhood house held a presence, and it wasn't a good one. In fact, my father shared with us a story that happened when we were children that validated the feelings we had about our house.

He recounted a tale wherein he awoke in the middle of the night by something he described as negative and with an agenda. He said he felt that the negative energy was headed into the bedroom my sister and I shared. He went in our bedroom to "protect" us from the energy.

That may have been the end of that story, but he's stated feeling that energy numerous times. This didn't surprise me; our house had much negative energy, which is what paranormal energies feed off of.

With our feelings and our father's, we were even more convinced the house held an energy that wasn't friendly.

Let's fast forward a couple of years. My sister, my mother, and I were home. My sister was coming down the hallway, which ended right in the middle of where our living room and kitchen branch off into their separate rooms. At this point in the house, one can see both into the living room and kitchen. As my sister started veering toward the kitchen, she asks my mother if my brother-a tall, lanky 20-something with long scraggly hair- was home, to which my mother said no. This confused my sister, who still swears to this day she saw our brother sitting in the living room right before she asked. He wasn't there when she went to verify her claim.

Again, let's fast forward a few more years to when my nephew, my sister's son, turned three. He would make it a point to stand in front of our hallways, and "bite" or yell at something down the hall. When asked what he was doing, he'd say he was playing, or in the case of yelling he was arguing, with Shawn. Though my sister and I had our concerns that this negative energy is the same one we felt when we were teens, we wrote it off as an imaginary friend of sorts.

However, my nephew started to mention how Shawn was now in their house, not in our family home. Shawn would be in his bedroom, "scaring him" to the point where he wouldn't sleep in his room without the lights on. He would often say Shawn was mean, and he wouldn't play in his playroom because Shawn was always there.

In my mind, Shawn had followed my nephew from our house to his, because their house was riddled with negative energy from an unhealthy living environment, again, what paranormal energies feed off of. I didn't mention this to my sister for fear of opening up a can of worms that weren't my business.

One day, my nephew was in his house, as my sister, her husband, and their friends came over and were talking outside. My nephew wanted to go outside too, but the moment he did he started screaming for my sister to hold him and take him back into the house. No one knew what was wrong with him, until he pointed to the tall, lanky, white T-shirt-clad, scraggly-haired friend of her husband and called him "Shawn."

I am now convinced the energy within my childhood home which clearly had a look to him, followed my nephew to his house due to it being a rich resource for negative energy from their family, and the family that lived there before them (it was her husband's childhood home). Perhaps it followed us to our home all those years ago because of our own negative energy, I will never know.

My nephew doesn't mention Shawn anymore, but can tell you who he was and the strife he brought him. Perhaps Shawn stayed in their old house because of its overabundance of negative energy. Perhaps Shawn was just an imaginary friend. I will never know this either, but what I do know is that these instances are too similar to be anything but paranormal.

OKLAHOMA

AS TOLD BY: Elizabeth Kiley

I moved out of the apartment on Lincoln Ave into a place near my brother's. It was a two bedroom upper duplex for nearly the same price as the one bedroom. I thought the layout was kind of strange, because when you came in you were at the back of the place and entered into the kitchen. There was a small bedroom straight ahead and to the left was the bathroom and the door to the living room. When you entered the living room to the right was another door to a huge bedroom with two big windows and it had two doors, a closet and steps to the attic. My daughter was about seven months old when we moved in and I thought with all the bright sunshine in the front bedroom that should be for her. I set up a bed and placed a dresser in the small bedroom for me and set up her crib and toys in the front. I always had a creepy feeling in the back bedroom so I just slept on the couch. I never even put my clothes back there. I really never had a problem except every now and then the kitchen faucet would turn on at strange hours of the night. I really liked having the attic space because there were clotheslines up there so I got a second hand washer and could hang clothes up there all year. No more Laundromats! The only other thing up there was a large old recliner.

Everything was going well and we were happy. Once my daughter started walking, she would go upstairs and I thought it was alright, but I would hear her talking up there with one of her books. When I asked her who she was talking to she said that grandpa was reading her a story. I thought that was funny, so I went up to check on her and there she was... sitting on the recliner and it was moved right by the steps. Looking back, I thought it was strange but I wasn't too concerned. She was barely two and weighed about twenty-five pounds, there was no way she could have moved it. I told her I would move the chair away from the steps, and that Grandpa could read better by the window.

I thought she just had a good imagination and it wasn't too far-fetched because her grandpa babysits her while I was at work. A few days went by and I was taking laundry up to hang and the chair was back next to the steps again! I asked my daughter how it got there. She said grandpa moved it. I thought she was talking about my dad so I let it go but I figured I' d talk to him Monday and have him stop. When Monday came, my Dad said he didn't know what I was talking about. He had never gone up there and he said he doesn't let my daughter up there either. So from then on I put a little slide lock high up on the door and left the chair by the steps. I was still comfortable in the house. It didn't seem like a bad spirit so I just left it well enough alone.

As time went by, I had met a man and after a while he wanted to get married and move in with us. My daughter was three when we were married and he came to live with us. Of course he didn't want to sleep on a couch, but he thought we should have the big bedroom and my daughter should be in back. I couldn't explain why we should just move instead but he wanted that big room. I had been there for almost three years and had not even opened that door since I put the bed and dresser in there. The first night she was in there was the most terrifying night of my life.

She went to be at 7:30 p.m. and at 9:00 p.m. she was screaming. I ran to her room and I couldn't get the door to open. She kept screaming and screaming and I couldn't get the door open. Finally, my husband opened the door, calmed her down and called me a weakling. He put her back to bed and I told him to leave the door a little open if it's that sticky and he did. At about 11:00 p.m. she started screaming again. I went to the door and it was shut tight! I tried to open it and it was totally stuck and she was still screaming. I yelled at my husband to open it and he came and couldn't get it. We didn't know what to do, we thought maybe she was blocking the door with a toy because it would open a little but not much. We finally got her calmed down and asked her what was in front of the door? To our surprise she said a bad-man put the dresser there! Just as she said it the kitchen faucet came on full blast. We pushed so hard and finally got it open, and sure enough the heavy chest was in front of the door. It was not on wheels, and she was three. I put her out on the couch for the rest of the night.

This finally made my husband realized we needed to move somewhere else, but with both of us working we really didn't have time. I moved the dresser in front of the door to pin it completely open and I put a hook lock to the window trim and locked it open. We would put her in the room at night to go to sleep, but every morning we found her on the couch.

I was coming home one day with her in the car and as I was opening the garage door I noticed my daughter waving at someone. I asked who she was waving to and her response was chilling. She told me it was grandpa from the attic. I looked up and there was a figure by the attic window. My daughter said she missed him since she's not allowed up to see him. Then she told me the man in her room is really a monster and he's mean. He hurts her and steals the covers so that's why she comes out on the couch. When I heard that I had had enough. I started looking for a new place and we moved the very next month.

All the way across the alley into a three-bedroom duplex because I was pregnant.

OREGON

AS TOLD BY: Bobbi Autry

About five years ago, a friend asked me to stay at his father's house in Independence, Oregon, while he was out of the country. There were animals to care for and some general farm work needed to be done. I agreed to stay and help, after all it was out in the country and it was a break from the city and a chance to have some quiet and relaxation. Or so I thought...

The first night I was sitting in the living room and the television was off, because I was making a pallet to sleep on the couch. I had just put the blanket down and was about to lie down, when I heard something outside. I sat down for a minute and just listened. It was definitely coming from right outside the window, so I pulled back the curtain to look. Of course, nothing was there. I laid back and listened for another 15 minutes, and looked again but there was nothing out there. The sounds that I was hearing, sounded like a horse and buggy perhaps, and it sounded like people were whispering or talking quietly. I decided to stay up because I was getting freaked out; I did not sleep until after the sun was coming out that morning.

When my friend came down from upstairs for coffee that morning after working a graveyard shift, I asked him what it was that I had heard in the night. He told me that I was not the first person to have heard that same thing. He then told me a story about something he and his girlfriend had experienced:

He said they were in the downstairs bedroom on the bed and it began to shake. It lifted about six to eight inches off the ground and then dropped. My heart was pounding and I was so scared I felt like I could not breath and right then the hair on the back of my neck stood on end; it was a very eerie feeling. I told him I could not stay out there anymore and I got in my car with my friend Adam and we headed down the long downhill driveway. I looked to the right of the drive and saw what looked to me like a soldier from the civil war era or something. It was about six feet tall and a bluish gray transparent figure wearing a coat with buttons down both sides of the chest, he was holding a rifle in one arm, and wore a hat with a small squared bill.

I sped up and left the drive as fast as I could, without saying a word. Down the road I stopped the car and turned to Adam, at that time he asked me if I had seen something at the bottom of the hill. When I didn't respond he explained the exact thing I had seen. I knew then that I was not losing my mind, it was really there. Needless to say, I did not go back after that day.

PENNSYLVANIA

AS TOLD BY: KATHLEEN GLATFELTER

For me, July 23, 1999 is a day like September 11, 2001... it is one of those days where I remember every single minute, though I wish I could forget. That was the day my world crashed around me.

At 11:30 a.m. that Friday morning, I invited a co-worker to lunch because I wanted to stop at a nearby flower shop to finalize my flowers for my upcoming wedding. We had lunch and went to the flower shop. My friend had just gotten a new convertible, and since it was a beautiful day we weren't in a hurry to get back to work. So I said, "Let's go this way, I'll show you where my mom lives."

I need to backtrack and say that this particular co-worker was usually not one I asked to lunch, although we got along fine, she was usually making sales calls and wasn't in the office much. And the restaurant we chose was not one I went to regularly when I was at work, it just happened to be near my florist.

So as we are nearing my old house, I saw ambulances and thought someone in the neighborhood had been hurt. The neighborhood was full of elderly people, and I hadn't lived there for some time, so I wouldn't have known who lived in the house where the ambulance was. As we got closer I knew who they were helping, my mother.

I frantically told my friend that it was my mom, and to go back to work and tell my fiancé to meet me at the hospital. The paramedics were about to bring my mother out. I stopped them and said I was her daughter, and they said something but in my frantic state I didn't know what it was. I told her, "I'm here now, you're going to be okay." Then I held her hand as they took her to the ambulance.

The ride to the hospital was so surreal. There were two ambulances, and they wouldn't let me in with her. So as I followed her ambulance, it seemed like we weren't going very fast at all, and I know the sirens were not on. I kept asking them, "Why aren't the sirens on?" to which they replied, "We're doing the best we can for your mom."

When we got to the hospital they put me in a room and wouldn't let me see her or tell me anything. My fiancé came, and then like on TV two doctors came into the room to talk to me and asked me to sit down. I knew what that meant, so I refused to sit down. I thought if I stood then they couldn't tell me anything, that she was going to be fine. My fiancé pulled me down and then they explained to us that there was nothing more they could do for her, she was gone.

She was only 50 when she died, so an autopsy was performed. It was determined that she had a massive heart attack and died instantly. The hospital said she died there, but I think she called me to her and held on until I arrived because I meant the world to her, and she to me. The day was too full of things that I didn't normally do for it to be any other reason. It also became known to me that she had called her boyfriend around 11am because she didn't feel well and wanted to go to the doctor. She didn't call me because she didn't want me to worry, but I couldn't have helped her anyway.

I still to this day believe that she visits me. I will smell smoke in my car when I'm the only one in it and she's the only one in my family who smoked. I'll see a butterfly at my windshield when I'm on the highway, yet it doesn't get smashed in my window. Things go missing in my house, and when I ask her if she is playing with me they'll appear again in a weird spot. And just now, I asked her to give me a sign if it was okay for me to share this story. My email is synced to my cell phone, so I said, "If it's okay with you Mom, send me a sign. Send me an email."

About five minutes later, I got one about a new follower on my blog.

RHODE ISLAND

AS TOLD BY: Nicholas Soucy

This was an experience I had the first night I moved into my new home. This detail is significant because spirits do not like intruders to live in the house they will always consider theirs. So for activity to happen on the first night is not uncommon. It was around 2:30 a.m. which is significant because all the unexplained events that happen in my home happen around this time. It started when I heard footsteps coming from my attic. The footsteps were pacing back and forth across the attic and it stopped on the right side of the attic. After it stopped I heard a loud thud, like someone had fallen down. After that the footsteps stopped.

Years later when I was remodeling the attic to make two bedrooms and a bathroom up there, I was removing old floorboards to install cables for the new rooms. As I cut out the floorboards I looked on the underside of them and noticed that under the floorboards was charred, suggesting that there was a fire at some point in the history of the house. This is significant because the side of the attic that the burnt floorboards were discovered, was the same side of the house that the footsteps stopped and the person could be heard falling. This suggests that the person was running around upstairs while possibly on fire and finally fell down dead.

When my upstairs project was finally completed, I took my dog up there to show him the new rooms. The dog suddenly lowered his head and started growling at a corner. My family and I watched him as he was growling at a seemingly empty corner of the room. This could not be explained logically, because two other family members and I were up in the room with the dog and we did not hear any noise or see anything in the corner. In all of the years I have lived in the house I have not heard any noise to suggest that any creature had taken residence in the attic like rats or any other animal that would cause my dog to act this way. This corner was also on the same side of the attic where the burnt floorboards where we heard the ghost fall. They say dogs can sense spirits that we cannot. Kind of like when dogs can hear noises that are below the range of human hearing. Maybe they can see or sense spirits that are below the light waves that we can see. Dogs can also see in the dark so maybe he saw something that we could not. Dogs usually act this way to protect their owners of things that would want to hurt us. We had found a dog leash under the floorboards while remodeling so maybe he was growling at the spirit of another dog.

The home where all of this happened was built in 1950 and there had been at least two other families that have lived there previously. While remodeling the attic we found a picture under the floorboards. The picture was of a big family and the picture was in black and white which suggests that the picture was of the family who originally lived there in the fifties. We bought the house from an elderly lady who had a ˙husband die in that house. This means that there has been at least one death in the house.

SOUTH CAROLINA

AS TOLD BY: Roderick Brehm

The first strange experience I remember having was around 1985-1986. I was about five years old (currently 31) and we lived in a trailer behind my late grandmother's house. I recall clearly, watching TV and playing in the living room, when I heard my house cat growling.

For reference we had one of the single-wide trailers which had a full glass window in the front.

My cat was solid white and genetically deaf, as some white cats are. He was in the front window staring out at something. As a curious child I went to go see what he was upset about. I ran up and pulled back the curtains to see some large creature, which looked like a hairless version of the old American Werewolf in London, walk around the front of my grandmother's house to the back. It walked on all four legs and I remember the eerie shine from its eyes. The head swayed similar to a bear, but its teeth were exposed which is not anatomically correct for a black bear or grizzly because they have lips.

The part that has always stood out most to me was its hairless features. If it was a dog, that was a scary looking, really messed up dog!

Normally you can chalk this up to be a child's bad dream, or maybe some other movie I watched, but we had physical evidence.

The poor thing urinated all over the front of the window area and Mom remembers cleaning it up. My mom also heard the cat screaming, literally screaming.

It was the most bizarre thing I have ever seen.

SOUTH DAKOTA

AS TOLD BY: Chris Becker

About 10 years ago, I had something very odd happen. I was at home and going to sleep.

I remember laying down and falling asleep. After I fell asleep, I randomly woke up. At first I wasn't sure what was happening, or where I was, much like when a person first wakes up. But then I realized, I was standing in the dining room of my house, in front of the sliding glass door.

As I was standing there, I realized I was staring at something big floating in the sky about 1000 feet from my house. I wouldn't say saucer shaped, but something like that. It's somewhat hard to describe. It seemed almost octagonal in shape, like a flying stop sign.

I stood there and stared for about half a minute. The next thing I know; I'm using the restroom. I remember doing that before going to bed though, which seemed odd. After I finished, I walked back to bed and laid down, but it felt like I had no control. I wanted to go back to the dining room, but couldn't.

I woke up the next morning, and my mom was asking me why I was in the kitchen by the door in the middle of the night. She said I stood there for a while, and then walked downstairs. I have no clue what it is that I saw, but I know I really saw it. I do know it was not an airplane, nor any other type of known aircraft. I am a production director for a local TV station and have been for a few years. I've only told a few people about it, them being close friends.

TENNESSEE

AS TOLD BY: Edward Kolnaski

Before we disembark on this journey through time, and Nashville, and the paranormal experiences revealed by the tour guide and my family, let me give you a little background into my family on my father's side. My grandparents met in Hawaii during World War II, my grandfather was an officer and a Navy LCT, my grandmother a Navy nurse. My grandmother was part of a nursing corps that bravely volunteered to investigate a mysterious illness that quarantined marines and sailors from the rest of the population for fear of pandemic. The illness ended up being a flu variation but she was commended for her valor. My grandfather participated in several combat beach landings, on one occasion, the ship next to his communications tower was destroyed by enemy mortar fire. Both returned healthy from the war and married and had four children. My father being the last.

My grandmother's parents immigrated from Ireland and Poland, my grandfather's both came from Poland. At a very young age my grandmother's mother passed away, leaving her to help her father raise five boys.

My aunts are all different and wonderful in their own ways. My Aunt Patty is the eldest and has three daughters. Her middle child is the reason we were vacationing in Tennessee. My Aunt Coraline came next, she has two daughters, both out of college and teaching at this point, her youngest, my cousin Robby, is probably my best and oldest friend. Then comes my Aunt Sally, the most eccentric of the family, yet also the quietest and humble. Perhaps eccentric isn't the right term, more like open minded. Her oldest, Will, is definitely eccentric, but also a world class story teller. Also probably my best friend. Willy has been a high school soccer star, MMA fighter, mixologist, a writer and currently works in Antarctica. He's a world traveler, with the craziest stories. A fan of fantasy stories from an early age he used to tell us he was an alien, or a vampire because he never slept. Big into philosophy and mysticism, Will always makes for great conversation. Recently he told me he was attempting to infiltrate a group of vampires. Bullshit, was my first reaction, but I egged him on to the disdain of my younger brother Tim, and my friend Nico, both trapped in the car with us on a five-hour drive back from Vermont.

Will has two younger siblings, both awesome in their own respects, but not as interesting as Will.

So here we are, the whole clan assembled in Nashville ready to embark on a spiritual journey through Nashville, hunting for the metaphysical remains of some of the cities former inhabitants. As I stated earlier we were waiting across from a hotel, that we weren't allowed to enter, but was reported to be haunted by a ghost of a beautiful woman, whose story for haunting the premises escapes me at the moment. What I remember is that at this point I was introduced to the orb, in regards to the paranormal. An orb is the captured image of a ghost or a spirit, according to our guide. He produced several pictures taken in and outside the hotel with orbs floating in them. I thought that was particularly cool.

As we traveled the streets we stopped at the Capitol Building, to try and catch a glimpse of the dead wife of Andrew Jackson, my favorite president. One other site was the back door of a nightclub, where a famous jazz club owner/ mobster was stabbed to death. Nothing here either. This whole time I was hoping to see something paranormal but doubted anything would animate before our eyes. Yet I still clung to the hope. I'm a rational person, but I believe that the world is more magical than we like to believe. I don't know if they exist, but I hope there are Bigfoot roaming our wilderness. I lived in Burlington, Vermont on Lake Champlain, and hoped I'd get to see the legendary Champ, a creature comparable to the Monster of Loch Ness. Therefore, I could confirm that there is indeed more to this world. As I grew increasingly bored by what became basically a roam around Nashville with my family, some strangers, and our bizarre, poorly dressed troop leader to the spirit world, I thought I'd have some fun with my Aunt Sally.

My Aunt Sally like her son Will, was a fan of fantasy novels, had an open mind, and according to my father was a hippy during the 60s. If anyone had thought they'd seen a ghost I was sure it would be her so, sick of listening to the guide and not finding a speck of evidence of paranormal activity, I approached my Aunt Sally. Our conversation went something like this.

"So Aunt Sally do you believe in ghosts?"

"Ya I think so."

"Have you ever seen a ghost before or anything like that?" Hoping please say yes.

"Well actually when I was a little girl..." Oh my god! I knew it! She's crazy, just like her son, I can't wait to hear what nonsense is going to come out of my Aunt's mouth. Who by the way is also a researcher for a leading pharmaceutical company.

"When we lived at the old house that your great granddad lived in I used to wake up at night, look down the hall and see a woman smoking a cigarette down in the living room. She was beautiful, wore a red dress, and would rock back and forth in her chair, always smoking a cigarette. I assumed it was a friend of my mother or father's, because they both never smoked, but didn't mind if others did in the house. But it was always so late."

I was dumbfounded, and at the same time a little underwhelmed by her story. I was hoping for something more fantastic, scarier, like Will and his vampire stories. This paranormal sighting was believable, but not the malevolent spirit, poltergeist type of story I was expecting.

"Wow that's interesting." I said, and left it at that.

Moving on to my Aunt Patty who is also my godmother, and an aunt I am very close with and like to joke around with. I was looking forward to telling her the story I had heard from her sister. Instead I asked her if she had ever saw a ghost or anything paranormal. Her reply was even more shocking.

"You're not going to believe me, but ya I think I did when I was a little girl at our old house on Traverse Street." My aunt is usually a very stoic, rational woman, and strictly Catholic. Her belief in ghosts extends as far as the Resurrection of the Savior, or so I assumed.

"My bed used to be placed against the wall facing the door, looking all the way down the hall. And when I was a kid I would sometimes wake up at night and see a woman in a red dress smoking cigarettes in a rocking chair. I always thought it was a dream but it happened more than once."

"Did my Dad see it too?" I wondered.

"I don't think so because your Dad was too young. We didn't live in that house when he was born, but you can ask him. It probably was just a dream but it was so real. She was so vivid. Extremely pretty too."

"Did you ever try and get up and talk to her?"

"No."

"Why?"

"I don't know I guess I was a little bit scared. And she was just sitting there all the time. So peaceful, smoking her cigarettes, reading a book. I guess I was scared or too tired."

Okay, now two out of three of my aunts have described strikingly similar descriptions of a paranormal experience. Before going onto my third aunt, Aunt Coraline, I talked to my Dad. "Hey you won't believe this, I just spoke with Aunt Sally and Aunt Patty about ghosts right. Well they both told me the exact same story! How crazy is that?"

"That's crazy." He said, clearly not as blown away as I was. So I moved on to Aunt Coraline.

"Hey Aunt Coraline."

"Hello Edward! Isn't this so much fun?"

"Ya. This city itself is awesome. I want to come back someday." Six years later and I have regrettably not been back.

"And so much history!" She knows I love history.

"Ya this is great. So Aunt Coraline, you ever see a ghost?" This was a sensitive subject. One that I hesitated to bring up because her husband, an uncle dear to my heart who died to young of a heart attack had passed away, widowing her about four years earlier at the age of fifty.

"Well you know what Eddie." Her voice got softer, almost to a whisper. "When I was little I used to have a room at the end of the hallway when you're Ant Patty moved into her other room at our old house. Do you remember that house?"

Not really, I thought, but what I said was, "Ya I remember it."

"I don't know if it was just a dream but I used to see a woman in a red dress with beautiful blonde hair sitting in the living room sometimes late at night."

"You sure it wasn't just Grandma." This was getting very eerie, but I felt part detective at this point, unraveling a decades old ghost story one witness at a time.

"I don't think so because her hair was so blonde and she was thinner than Grandma, but with a similar face."

"This is crazy. Have you ever told Aunt Patty or Aunt Sally about this?"

"No."

"Why not?"

"I'm not sure, I guess I didn't think much of it, that it was just a dream."

"I don't think it was a dream." I told her.

"Because they all just told me that exact same story."

Immediately she called back to her sister Patty, who was walking towards the back of the tour with my mother. Then she got her other sister, my Aunt Sally and the shared their experiences. All had the same experience except my Aunt Coraline remembered one night where the beautiful stranger in the house looked up at her, causing her to close her eyes, but when she opened them again, the woman in red was still there, smiling at her from her chair in the living room. The specter no longer frightened them, in fact it never did. The sight of this mysterious woman in their home was a surprise to all of them, but also calming at the same time. Before the tour was done we speculated that it could possibly be a glimpse of my great grandmother, who died when my

Grandma was very young. Her cause of death, lung cancer.

TEXAS

AS TOLD BY: Elise Reeves

Several years ago, my family was staying at my grandparent's house for the Easter holiday. The first night we were there, I had a spooky but harmless experience that I was eager to tell my family about the next morning. The drawers of my dresser had mysteriously opened up by themselves and my grandparents had awoken to find a brown substance smeared across the counter-tops in the kitchen. Nobody could explain where the brown stuff came from or what it even was. While we were all speculating about what it could be, my grandmother told me that I needed to talk my cousin, about what happened when she was in high school.

My cousin, who will be called Lauren, lived far out in the country on a big farm in south Texas. The house was set back from the road, with a long dirt driveway leading up to it. There were two very tall, and very old oaks trees that grew right by the driveway. All the cousins would spend the days climbing the trees and swinging on the rope swings that hung from the branches.

The house itself had been built on the property when Lauren's parents were first married. Lauren stayed in the same bedroom for her whole life. Nothing strange ever happened to her until she was early into high school. She would hear something tapping on her windows all night long. When she would finally fall asleep, she dreamt that two Native American men would be outside her windows, tapping on the glass and trying to find a way inside. Eventually, one of the men would find a way to open her windows, crawl inside her room and he would force her out of her bed and take her outside. He would then drag her across the yard to where the oak trees grew by the dirt driveway. To her horror, the man would rape her beneath the oak trees. After that, she would dream that she was back in her room and the second Native American man was there with her. He took her by the hand and led her through the house until they were in her parents' room. She always saw the same thing; her parents were in their bed, dead.

This happened to her night after night. The dream was the same every single time. There was always the constant tapping on her windows, then the terrible nightmares. After months of being tormented in her sleep, Lauren finally began to sleep on the couch. Her mother always assumed that Lauren fell asleep watching television or something along those lines. She didn't know the true reason behind Lauren's new sleeping habits.

Lauren spent the rest of high school sleeping on the couch. She could not bring herself to spend another night in her room, and she was too scared to tell people what was happening to her. She was too afraid that nobody would believe her, or that people would think she was crazy.

During the last few years that Lauren was living at home, her brother brought home a new girlfriend. This girl was invited to stay the night and she slept in Lauren's unoccupied room.

The next morning, the girl was talking to Lauren over breakfast and she asked what was wrong with her room. Lauren, never having told anybody about the dreams, asked her what she was talking about. The girl began to tell Lauren about the loud tapping on the windows before she fell asleep, then she said that she had a terrible nightmare about two Native American men coming into her bedroom and doing things to her.

Lauren was shocked that this girl was having the same experience as her after spending only one night in her room. She finally admitted to what she had been going through for years and explained that because of the dreams, she spent her nights on the couch.

The girl claimed to be an amateur clairvoyant and said that there were some possible explanations for her nightmares. She felt that there were two angry spirits that were trying to warn her of danger if she continued to live in her room. The first one would take her and rape her beneath the trees and the second one would show her the consequences if she stayed.

Several years passed after that incident. Lauren moved out and was attending college, no longer living in the house.

One day a man drove up to the house and asked Lauren's mother if he could look at the property. With him he had documents proving that his ancestors once lived on the land. He specifically wanted to see the two old oak trees. When he was at the spot between the trees, he told my Aunt that some of his family was buried beneath the spot.

It was the very same spot where Lauren was raped every night in her dreams.

Lauren's mother was shocked. The man went on to say that the most of the land was where a tribe of Native Americans lived and that somewhere on the property was a sacred burial site.

Lauren's mother never told him about the connection between the dreams and the Native Americans and the spot between the oak trees, so he left and they never saw him again.

To this day nobody knows why the spirits of the Native American men came to Lauren in her dreams and caused her harm. All we know is that they wanted to hurt her, and they wanted her gone.

Lauren, now happily married and starting her own family, has never again spent another night in her old room. She claims that people who sleep there say that they experience strange things; the old tapping on the window, seeing shadows walk down the hallway, and the general feeling of something being there that they can't see. However, nobody but her or the clairvoyant girl has ever had the nightmares.

She jokingly offered for me to stay to sleep over and see for myself, if I didn't believe her.

UTAH

AS TOLD BY: JUSTUS THOMAS

It was a warm summer night and Tanner and I had nothing to do. Our usual trio, Tanner, Caiden, and myself had been watching at least four horror movies every week for almost the entire summer. We had become connoisseurs of the supernatural. We watched ghost hunting TV shows and documentaries about horrific events and places. We slept by the river and told stories of creatures lurking in the dark trees around us. We walked the city at night and searched for places that may have been occupied by unseen beings... factories, abandoned houses, farms, and ancient schoolhouses. We had reached a point where we craved fear, and our rapid consumption of horror movies had built up our tolerance to the point where nothing we watched impressed us. So on this night, feeling we may never know fear again, Tanner and I got in my car and drove, with no intentions whatsoever.

"Want to go drive through Benjamin?" I asked. "We could go look at the Benjamin House or something." "I don't care," Tanner said in a disinterested tone. "Let's just cruise around."

I turned up my stereo, the permanent home of a Kavinsky album I had burned onto a CD myself, and to the haunting vintage beats of the french electronic musician, we slipped through the night air. The headlights of my little car illuminated the advancing road, completely devoid of any cars or life. We slowed down as we passed the "haunted" old Benjamin House. I had been in it before and decided it was just an old broken house.

"Should we stop and check it out?"

Seconds after I said this, a police car drove slowly down the road. It was a popular spot for teenage mischief and practitioners of the occult, and the owners often asked for a patrol car to drive by and make sure no one was meddling. For obvious reasons, we decided not to visit the Benjamin House that night. We were silent as I navigated the dark streets of the farming community, turning at random, going down streets we've never been down before. I didn't have a single thought about where I was driving or what my destination was.

I remember reaching what I thought was a dead end, my headlights illuminating the remnants of an ancient garage or shed, half hidden in trees, neighbored by an un-lit house in the same condition.

"Dude...this is..." I started.

"Freaking creepy..." Tanner finished.

Normally we would have left the car and explored, but as soon we saw those dilapidated structures, the peaceful feelings of the night were replaced with a twisting anxiety, an oppressive force, like two magnets with the same charge being pushed closer and closer together. I realized the dead end actually had a small road to the left.

"Should we keep following this road?" I inquired slowly.

"It will probably be faster," Tanner said. "I think the main road is somewhere over there," gesturing in the direction of the rotted shed.

I nodded and turned onto the road. As we drove, I felt the uneasiness and the uncomfortable force on my throat start to increase.

"Do you feel that, in your throat?" I asked.

"Yeah," Tanner replied, "and in your-"

"Chest and stuff?" I exclaimed, "Yes! What the heck man, what's going on?"

"I don't know!"

We were grinning from ear to ear. We had finally found our fear fix. I slowed to a stop and rolled down the windows. To either side, there were apparently abandoned houses. Dark windows and unkempt yards adorned every one.

I started to speak, "This is the weirdest-".

"Where are all the lights?" Tanner interrupted.

I looked to the east, expecting to find the lights of Spanish Fork and Provo, nothing. I looked up and down the street, searching for a streetlight, I saw none. The only light came from the car's headlights. This entire time we had been parked in the center of the road, engine idling. I slowly let off the clutch and eased into the gas. Our car crawled past the empty houses that were filled with things that did not want us there. The pressure on my throat had been steadily increasing, I could tell by the way Tanner was holding his own throat that he was experiencing the same effect. The air was dead. The only sound cutting through the night was my 1999 Hyundai Elantra's small engine. The only lights that we could see were the headlights, the city lights we had always been able to see from anywhere else in Benjamin were nowhere to be found. I turned off the lights, slowly passing the houses one by one.

I turned to my passenger with a grin and choked out, "Where are we?".

"Something is just off about these..." said Tanner.

"I know," I replied, "why do they all look abandoned? I didn't even know this road was here. And why do I feel like something is pushing on my throat?".

"It's getting harder to breathe."

I stared into the empty windows, searching for any sign of life, of anything that could hate us this much. It felt like I was in the center of a room filled with people who hated me. Wherever we were, we were not welcome there. The pressure on my throat was beginning to become extremely uncomfortable. "Is this just a placebo thing?" I asked, putting a hand on my throat, "Are we just doing this to ourselves?"

"I don't think so," was his simple reply.

We had passed the houses and were now surrounded by fields completely devoid of life. The forceful opposition had been escalating, reaching a point where I was no longer excited about finding this truly fearful place. I started to speed up, this place was wrong. Abstract thoughts ran rampant in my mind, all playing on one theme: you are not welcome here. I switched the lights back on and shifted into second gear, no longer able to stand our confident crawling speed. I shifted into third and saw a street light in the distance. I focused on the street light, and as we approached I felt the pressure on my throat begin to lift. Now I raced towards the street light, and saw that it illuminated a cross roads. The euphoric rush that comes after true fear hit me like freight train.

"What the-"

"Did you feel-"

"Where-"

We reacted as only true horror junkies could, we were thrilled to finally have an experience that frightened us. I turned left at the street light. I could see the lights of the neighboring cities in the distance. Normal looking houses lined the street, and the hateful force had disappeared completely. "I can't wait to tell Caiden about this!" exclaimed Tanner.

I was grinning as I replied, "We have to take him back there! That was literally the scariest thing I have ever experienced!"

"What do you think it was? Ghosts? Demons? Slenderman?" he asked.

I laughed, "Whatever it was, I don't think it liked us very much."

"We should go back," Tanner said thoughtfully, "see if we feel that again. I want to know if we were just scaring ourselves, or if there actually was something."

"Replicate the results," I said, "good idea. We should have a ghost hunting show."

I turned the car around and headed back in the direction we had come from. I didn't recognize any of the houses.

"Did I make a wrong turn?" I said, "I don't remember any of these."

"Me either...I know this is the right road though. We never turned off of it."

We finally found the cross roads and turned back onto the street that didn't want us there.

"Is this th-" before I could finish, the choking feeling returned. Not as forceful as it was earlier, but definitely familiar. We smiled at the results of our experiment.

"But wait, I don't recognize any of these houses..." Tanner said.

They were in the same style as those that littered the sides of the first street, and they felt just as wrong, but they were placed differently. Yards littered with different garbage, fields in a different order.

Just as I said, "Neither do I," the street kicked us out onto a road that I knew would take us home. The milder feeling of oppression disappeared. I was baffled.

"Let's just go home. We'll figure this out later," said Tanner.

"I concur."

We returned a week or so later with Caiden, eager to show him the street. We drove around the tiny farming community of Benjamin for hours before finally giving up. It was gone. And although it had frightened me more than any other experience of my life up to that point, I missed it. It had satisfied that craving for the supernatural that nothing before or since has been able to match. Ever since I've been watching for wrong places, wrong people, wrong things, things that just don't belong. Fear isn't chainsaws and zombies; it isn't gore or twisted killers. It simply comes from things that are wrong.

VERMONT

AS TOLD BY: JOSH MASON

My mom passed away on December 25th, 2005 and my best friend, on March 29th, 2006.

A week before my friend was killed in an accident due to drunk driver. I had gone to bed and everything was normal I fell fast asleep into a dream.

I was in a big truck on the highway and we got in an accident. Everything went black and then I was screaming, "We killed someone! We killed someone," and then I woke up but not really: I sat up in my bed and looked over to my office (which is connected by double doors to my bedroom) and my mom stood there surrounded by bright white light.

She's looking at me and walking around to my side of the bed. I scooted over to the middle of my bed and my mom got in, placing her hands together as if to pray as she laid beside me. She slept with me that night and when morning came, I woke up suddenly sitting up gasping for air in the center of my bed.

My friend's name was Shanna, and I remember telling her about my experience two days after. We shared the same thoughts: someone I loved was going to get killed in an accident. Seven days after my mom came to me I received a phone call at 11p.m. Shanna had gotten into an accident with her boyfriend in his truck. She was killed instantly but he walked away with not even a scratch. The accident in my dream took place directly to the left of where Shanna was killed.

VIRGINIA

AS TOLD BY: Rachael Queen

When I was a young girl, one of my biggest fears was that my toys would come alive and torment me somehow. I had no basis for this fear; I was just terrified of the concept that something I trusted so much to just be inanimate would, for some reason, suddenly animate itself.

Toys and dolls are a kid's best friends; constant inanimate companions. Mine went with me everywhere, I had at least one doll or stuffed animal with me at all times. Every day, I would spend hours playing with my toys. Sometimes by myself, sometimes with my brothers or some friends, but the toys were always with me. At night, though, I would lie awake in terror that something might happen. I was scared that, maybe out of the corner of my room, I might hear a voice.

Maybe something would creep up onto my bed. Maybe my hand would drop while I was sleeping and I'd be awoken to something grabbing it. After a couple of years, though, this fear subsided as I realized it wasn't actually going to happen to me and I was just being paranoid. At least, so I thought.

One morning, when I was in first grade, I awoke to someone shaking me. My mother would wake me up some mornings by lightly shaking my shoulder, so I thought that maybe it was her and that she was just annoyed with me for some reason. I couldn't have been more wrong. Fearing nothing, I began to open my eyes to this new day and was suddenly paralyzed with fear. Staring back at me were two sets of eyes, lifeless in appearance but clearly full of life. They belonged to two stuffed Teddy bears of mine. One was an orange bear, very cheery in appearance with a bright blue ribbon around his neck. The other was your average bear, brown and rather boring, but very fluffy and fun to cuddle.

Never again. I remained silent in my terror, realizing that my worst nightmares had come true just when I had finally started to accept how ridiculous they were.

They kept shaking me and began to half-sing, half-scream at me "Wake up Rachael! Wake up Rachael! Wake up!"

I was petrified, afraid to scream or talk or make any sort of noise because my six-year-old mind was utterly convinced that any sound from me would only make the situation worse. I did what any child, defenseless and completely out of their comfort zone, would do: I tried to hide under my covers and wait for it all to go away. I forced my eyes shut and told myself that this nightmare was just that, a nightmare.

No matter what I told myself, though, the situation did not become any less real. All I could do was wait. They got louder and louder and started shaking me more and more violently until, finally, it all came to an abrupt end.

I peeked out of my blanket and saw that they had become toys once again, lifeless and collapsed upon my bed. I immediately located scissors in my room and took to dismembering them, paying special attention to the heads. I wanted to be absolutely sure that this would never happen to me again. I took all of the pieces outside and threw them away; luckily it was garbage pickup day. My parents questioned me later about strange noises from my room that morning, but I simply told them that I had just been playing. I never told them or anyone the truth. Everyone would think I was crazy.

WASHINGTON

AS TOLD BY: Jason Buchko

Even as a little kid of seven, I knew about my past life. I would have very vivid dreams about it, even though I was too young to know what they meant. My parents raised me as a Christian, so going to them about this type of thing wasn't going to produce an answer that would satisfy me. I made it my life's hobby to research past lives. I also vowed to keep it to myself, as nobody would understand at best. The straightjacket would come at worst.

I had my dreams about the past that always felt more real than the other 'mundane' dreams. I was a soldier with a secret. The border town we laid siege upon was a place I once called home. I had a wife and daughter in there, of which their discovery would lead to my execution as well as their torture. In the final battle, I found them in the chaos. It was during our brief reunion that my captain came upon us. Knowing the agony and horrific acts that would befall my family if I didn't act quickly, I raised my sword and struck both of them down. I was commended for my actions by the captain, and our forces proceeded to eliminate the entire population of the town. Genocide with tear-filled eyes at its finest. Their faces haunted me for countless years.

Fast forward many years from my childhood. I had gotten married to a wonderful woman who had an open mind to these types of ideas. However, I hadn't thought of how to share with her my knowledge. That is when we found the old Ouija board. I must have bought it years before, but had no recollection of doing so. My wife became very interested in it, and of course wanted to try it out. I told her that there was prep work to be done, candles and such, and we would do it at midnight for best results.

With the candles lit around us, we both touched the planchette on the board in front of us. And then... nothing. Not a single peep. "Isn't it supposed to start moving?" my wife questioned. I told her that maybe we weren't concentrating hard enough, and for us to close our eyes and think mystical-type thoughts. That brought a chuckle, but she did as she was told. I closed my eyes, and did the same when I all of a sudden got a vision that I hadn't seen for many years. Tears started welling in my eyes when the planchette on the board started to move. I quickly choked back the welling as I opened my eyes and watched the window in the planchette spell out a single word. My name. My past name.

My wife quickly got excited in feeling the planchette move across the Ouija board for the first time. Then puzzlement crossed her face. "Thurin? What does that mean?" In my shock, I said nothing.

My face must have told a story, because "You know what it is, don't you?" were the next words I heard. I then told her that it was my name in a past life, but I hadn't told anybody about that, including her. "Oh, maybe this person knew you back then? We have to find out!" Our fingers graced the planchette a second time.

5

JOB NOT DONE

5

HERE

5

YOU FIND AGAIN

29

D

And that was it. We tried again to get more, but there was no movement to be had from it. My wife asked "Well, what does that mean? The only thing I can figure out is 29, and that's how old we will be next year. But the rest? What job? Find who? This doesn't make any sense." I had no answers for her. I had my own questions, but I needed time to ponder upon the meaning of it all. And what was the vision I had right before all of this happened? I wanted to go to bed, where I did my best thinking. However, my wife was wide awake at that point, and said she would have to do something in order to be sleepy. We made love, which seemed to accomplish more goals than were intended.

We tried the Ouija board the next night, but nothing would move. The next night produced the same results. "Maybe we broke it?" I told her that the reason it was in a long-forgotten box in the first place was because it never had worked for me in the past. I figured it was a piece of junk, but hated to throw away something I had paid good money to buy. So, back in the box it went, and we went on with our normal lives. We had tried a while later, but still the thing would not move for us.

What the sickness in the morning might not have told us, the pregnancy test had confirmed. We were going to have our first child. We were very excited, and she immediately went shopping to prepare for the day. In the back of my mind though, I did the math. Our child was conceived on that day the Ouija board came to life. You don't suppose...? Nah! Probably just a fluke. Everything will be just fine! And it was. The pregnancy went along without a hitch, and then the day came when we had to rush to the hospital for The Day.

After my daughter was cleaned up from her emerging into this world, I was given my new bundle to hold for the first time. That was when the realization hit me like a truck. I knew who the face was in my vision. I knew what the message from that night of the Ouija board meant. I immediately knew what job was left unfinished, and why it was of such vital importance. I looked into my daughter's eyes. The same eyes of the 5-year-old daughter I had lost so long ago. D... Daddy.

WEST VIRGINIA

AS TOLD BY: Olivia Powell

I moved to a small apartment in a town called Bellview. I worked a lot and my boyfriend worked out of town most of the time. One night, I was home alone laying on the couch, watching TV, just relaxing. My hair was draped over the side of couch and I started feeling something playing with my hair, deliberately. I thought it was my cat but I looked down at my feet, and she was laying there, looking at me, eyes wide. I got a really creepy feeling, and tried to sit up. Whatever it was pulled me back down by my hair and then, it was just gone.

About a week later, I was in the shower before meeting a friend for dinner. I was facing the water, my eyes closed. I turned around, so the water was running down my back and opened my eyes. For a brief second I thought I had seen a face, but I racked it up to the steam messing with my eyes. I was looking through my shower curtain, which was a thick mesh, but you could see out of it a little. I saw movements outside of the curtain. I moved a little closer, and a face, was right up against the curtain, less than inches from mine. It was a man, a bit older, maybe in his 40s. His face was twisted, almost in agony. I pushed the curtain out, toward his face, jumped out of the shower, threw on whatever I could find and left the apartment.

My boyfriend who is not a believer whatsoever, often asked me odd questions about things that happened in the night... but refused to answer any questions.

On the day we moved out of that apartment, I asked my landlord if we needed to pay to have the carpet replaced. She said "No, it was replaced right before you moved in, after Mr. so-and-so, killed himself." I looked at her and said, "You mean to tell me someone was killed in the apartment you let me rent?" She started to back pedal but I handed over my keys and got into my U-haul and drove almost 14 hours to South Carolina, where I am originally from.

WISCONSIN

AS TOLD BY: Elizabeth Kiley

The first one happened when I just had my first child. I had moved into a small one-bedroom apartment for cheap rent with heat included. I thought it was a great bargain. I had a nice family across the hall and we all soon became great friends.

As spring went to summer and summer to fall it started getting colder and colder there. My baby's hands were really cold one night and the landlord insisted that the heat was coming but we were cold. I decided to fire up the gas oven in the kitchen just to warm it up. I had never turned on the oven because I was raised with an electric stove so I had just been using an electric skillet to cook most everything.

I was watching TV in the bedroom and the stove was directly in front of me in the next room and my baby was finally warm enough to sleep.

I had set the oven to broil and had the door open so I was feeling pretty good until I saw this face in the oven! It was a bald man with a small narrow mustache and a round face! I was completely freaked out. He was smirking at me like I've never seen before and his eyes were black. I got up, turned on all the lights, kicked the door shut on the stove, and he was gone!

The baby was still asleep and I noticed it was 2:22 a.m. I sat there the rest of the night guarding my baby with one hand on the lamp and my knees tucked up under my chin.

The next day I told my neighbor what had happened and she said, "Oh, you met Frank?" I asked who Frank was and she told her daughter to go upstairs and get the pictures.

When she brought them down I could not believe it, it was definitely him! Then she told me about the people who lived in that apartment before they did, because the stove was originally in their apartment.

Frank had five kids and no money. He had been robbing places and got caught, he was awaiting his trial and was probably going to jail. He became very depressed and had closed all the doors to the kitchen and turned on the gas and killed himself.

She told me when the stove was in her apartment the gas would turn on by itself and the pilots always kept going out and she would smell gas all the time. The landlord finally got her a different stove but put that one in the unit I was in now.

I didn't know what to do; but I wasn't staying. I kept looking at that picture and on the back it said his full name, birth date, and Feb 22, 1975, his time of death – 2:22.

I was so fast to pack and start looking for a different place. I started staying with my brother at his apartment until I found a place and I never spent another night there. My landlord was complaining that I had only given him a 10-day notice till I moved and was threatening to keep my security deposit.

I told him he had better give it all back to me and get rid of that stove before Frank kills somebody! I got all of my security back and I was gone.

According to my neighbors, I wasn't the first or last to leave suddenly.

WYOMING

AS TOLD BY: LORI HUDSON

It was the fall of 2006 when I had to say goodbye to my 72-year-old dad. He had been through months of chemotherapy and we all knew it was only a matter of time before we would no longer have this wonderful man in our lives. It was October 19th, 2006 when I got the call that he had passed on. Although I had braced my heart months ago for this moment, somehow I still wasn't ready, I was absolutely devastated.

Up until this point in my life my parents had never raised me in the church or to practice any other kind of religion so I was an atheist. Not a devil worshiper, Satanist, or anything like that, but just believed that whenever we died we would simply decompose in the ground. It was a harsh reality to believe I would never see my dad again.

Every year since his death, October 19th has been a hard day for me. So one October night, very close to the five-year anniversary of his death he was heavy on my heart. I can't remember the exact date of this experience but I will surely never forget it.

As a little girl my dad would always sit on the corner edge of my bed and read me a bedtime story.

I will never forget waking up and seeing my dad sitting on the edge of the bed. He wasn't the sick old man with cancer I last remembered seeing, this was the handsome young man I remember sitting at the edge of my bed reading me a bedtime story. I went from being very groggy to sitting up wide awake. I even rubbed my eyes just to be sure I wasn't dreaming. He smiled at me and told me he was in a better place and not to be sad anymore, that I would see him again one day, and just like that he was gone.

I sat there in shock for a couple of minutes, still in disbelief of what had just happened. It had all just happened so quickly! I woke my husband up shortly after and told him what happened. I could tell he was happy for me but wanted to go back to sleep, but at that point I was wide awake.

To this day I still yearn for my dad to come see me again. Since then I have not seen him, but I know it was real. I don't go to church but now I know in my heart without a doubt, there is life after death and I can't wait to see my father again.

MEGAN'S EXPERIENCE

Sleepovers. What a great time for girls to get together and gossip, pig out on junk food, and give each other makeovers. All of that was done one night in the summer of 2005 at my friend Beth's house, but this one particular sleepover would be one we would never forget.

There were a bunch of girls over for the first part of the night. We had gone swimming, eaten pizza, and played some sort of board game. We had such a great time but around 9 all of the girls left. I was the only one spending the night that night because in the morning we had planned to go feed the homeless with our church group early the next morning. We had gone up to her room to change into our pajamas and gossip.

I don't remember how it came up but we had somehow got on the subject of ghosts. Beth was talking about how she had seen some episode on the "Maury Povich" show where they had shown footage of unexplainable things happening in people's homes. I told her it was all staged, because at that point I was a non-believer. She told me I was crazy to not believe in spirits. I remember smirking and then I came up with a challenge.

I remember so vividly sitting in her bed challenging any "ghost" to appear if they were real. We sat in silence and nothing happened. She told me we had to turn the lights off first if we wanted a ghost to appear. So we switch off the lights and again nothing happened for about ten minutes before I told her we were being ridiculous. So we moved on to our next topic of the night which probably had something to do with boys. Before we knew it, it was a little after 1 a.m. and we decided since we had to be up at 6 a.m. that we better hit the hay.

Beth was spoiled to a really nice bedroom. It was huge with a lot of space and her own private bathroom directly attached to her room. Right before you walked into her bathroom there was a large window. I remember laying on my back zoning out, looking at her bathroom thinking how lucky she was. I had to share a bathroom with my younger brother and older sister and it was half the size of hers. As I was laying there in my own pitiful jealousy I will never forget what I saw.

Right in front of her bathroom and window appeared this hovering ghost-like figure. It had no arms or legs from what I could tell it looked like a sheet with a hood and no face. Where the face was supposed to be it was completely dark. I was paralyzed with fear I could not move, I felt like I could hardly breathe. Only hours before I had mocked the spirit world and now they were coming after me.

Although it didn't physically cause me any harm it had already done enough psychological damage.

I remember staring at it for what seemed like forever but was probably no more than 45 seconds. Now that I knew I wasn't crazy I wanted to get Beth's attention. Like I said it felt like everything on my body was paralyzed except my eyes. So I stared at her hoping to get her attention. I will never forget she had her headphones in and she was listening to her Zune. When I finally got her attention she gave me a strange look. She knew something was wrong and asked me if I was okay. I looked back towards the window and as she followed my eye movement she too was struck with horror. Unlike me, she screamed and immediately jumped out of bed to turn on the lights and burst into tears.

After calming her down she blamed me for inviting the ghost into her home. She thought that her house would be forever haunted because I taunted the spirit world. I was still in so much shock about what I had just seen I was completely out of words to say. She asked me if I wanted to sleep in her big brother's room and I told her I would rather not because he smelled funny. Agreeing with me she told me we had to sleep with the lights on, and I agreed.

Although we didn't see the ghost again that night we both had a very hard time falling asleep that night. Needless to say we were both very tired the next morning as we were only running on two hours of sleep.

To my knowledge she has never seen the apparition again and luckily neither have I.

You can call it what you want but I have no doubt in my mind that "ghosts", "spirits", "apparitions", "visions", "souls" do live among us here on earth. Do I know their purpose or why they are here? No. But I'm sure one day we will all know the secrets to what goes on in the afterlife.

YOU MIGHT ALSO ENJOY...

Where are they from?
What do they look like?
What do they want from us?

These are common questions people ask when dealing with the possibilities of alien existence. We've all been curious at one point or another about what exists beyond planet Earth.

This book contains remarkable unexplained events that have taken place all over the United States of America. This collection holds fifty stories, one from each individual state. Each tale vastly different and unique from anything you've read before.

This is no ordinary book about extra-terrestrials...

You will unravel stories that expand your mind even further beyond the idea of abductions, mutilations, and crop circles.

Inside there are a couple of stories of missing people never found who loved ones believe have been abducted and taken to different planets. In another blurb, read about a woman who is certain her child is half human/half alien. A story impossible to forget is the fable of a man and his wife who raised an alien child for 6 years. Explore in detail about a young woman who swears she had a strange sexual encounter with the fourth kind. You will even read a love story that is (literally) out of this world, and many, many more interesting stories.

Whether you are an abductee, skeptic, researcher, or just want an interesting story to tell around the camp fire; this book is for you.

Don't miss this opportunity to read about people's beliefs, theories, and encounters that opened up their minds and forever changed their lives.

Made in the USA
Las Vegas, NV
05 March 2021